Charles de Salaberry

Soldier of the Empire, Defender of Quebec

by J. Patrick Wohler

Dundurn Press
Toronto and Charlottetown
1984

Editor: Robert Billings
Design and production: Ron and Ron Design Photography
Typesetting: Q Composition Incorporated
Printing: Marquis Printing Canada

The publication of this book was made possible by support from several sources. The author and publisher wish to acknowledge the generous assistance and ongoing support of the Canada Council and the Ontario Arts Council.

J. Kirk Howard, Publisher

Published by
Dundurn Press Limited
P.O. Box 245, Station F
Toronto, Canada
M4Y 2L5

Canadian Cataloguing in Publication Data
    Wohler, J. Patrick
        Charles de Salaberry, Soldier of the Empire, Defender of Quebec

(Dundurn lives)
Bibliography: p.
Includes index.
ISBN 0-919670-77-6 (bound). – ISBN 0-919670-76-8 (pbk.)

1. Salaberry, Charles Michel d'Irumberry de, 1778–
1829. 2. Canada – History – War of 1812 – Biography.*
3. Soldiers – Canada – Biography. 4. Great Britain.
Army – Officers – Biography. I. Title. II. Series.

FC443.S25W64 1984   971.03′4′0924   C84-099151-7
E353.1.S25W64 1984

Charles de Salaberry

Soldier of the Empire, Defender of Quebec

by J. Patrick Wohler

Contents

Illustrations and Photographs

Charles de Salaberry

The de Salaberry Coat of Arms with the motto given by Henry of Navarre.

Preface

As a young student of history, I was intrigued by a two and a half line reference to the victory at Chateauguay in 1813. I had to find out more about the Canadian commander, Charles de Salaberry; who he really was, where he had come from, what other soldiering he had done, and what happened to him after Chateauguay.

For several years, I was able to devote much of my time to this pursuit; haunted libraries and archives, visited sites in the Chateauguay and Richelieu valleys associated with de Salaberry, corresponded with a variety of individuals and institutions with related interests, and searched through museum collections for relevant artifacts.

But there were more demands on my time and other research to be done; the de Salaberry project slipped into the background but was not forgotten. The files continued to grow as information was uncovered, and anyone I met who might have something to offer on the subject was certainly asked to help. By the summer of 1979, the opportunity arose to set about re-analyzing the data and re-checking the historicity of the sources and write.

My research led me much farther afield than I had anticipated. The de Salaberry family tree can be traced back to medieval times – in fact, to Merovech (d. 457) who was the founder of the Merovingian dynasty. The family's strong military tradition was earned on countless battlefields and gun decks of a frequently turbulent world. After the family's arrival in Canada, there was scarcely a major campaign in which a de Salaberry did not take part.

Charles, himself, served in the British army and saw active service in the West Indies, Europe, and Canada. The highlight of his military career was a victory over disproportionate odds at Chateauguay in 1813.

There is so much worth telling in the story of the whole de Salaberry family that it became increasingly difficult to set the parameters for this work. However, I had set out to discover more about Charles, so I tried to adhere to that goal. I have brought in other elements only to the extent that I feel they help to know and understand him. But I also hope that through this story I can impart to the reader the realization that, hidden behind the staid recital of political and economic developments, the history of Canada has its fair share of drama, excitement, heroes, and villains.

So many people helped lighten the burden of research through their own published works, by directing me to sources, and sharing their own knowledge, that it is not possible fully to acknowledge them all individually. A few, however, must be singled out because of the invaluable nature of their assistance. Michel Brunet, the Assistant Dominion Archivist, was very helpful in both sharing his own knowledge of the family and in directing my research in the vast manuscript holdings of the Public Archives of Canada, including the *de Salaberry Papers*. *La Famille d'Irumberry de Salaberry* by Pierre-Georges Roy was a constant guide to the intricacies of the family's genaeology. The researcher's great friends, the librarians, never let me down and I called on their help in so many libraries in Montreal, Ottawa and elsewhere. The Historical Section of the Canadian army was also exceptionally helpful, and I am very grateful to the Montreal Military and Maritime Museum for kindly allowing me access to their archival material on de Salaberry. Parks Canada and particularly René Chartrand, military curator, were very helpful in providing advice and illustrations.

To the many who wrote or helped prepare the works listed in the bibliography my most sincere thanks for your help.

From the very beginning I have been strongly supported by a most understanding family, who not only encouraged but also participated in the work.

Needless to say, the responsibility for such short-comings as this book might possess is exclusively mine.

J. Patrick Wohler.

The Chateau d'Irumberry de Salaberry as it appears today.

Chapter One

What's in a Name?

A Family is Born

Battle honours and military service are a well established de Salaberry tradition. After the family's arrival in Canada there was scarcely a major campaign in which a de Salaberry did not take part. They fought the British Navy in King George's War (War of the Austrian Succession), and the Seven Years' War. They fought Montgomery and marched with Burgoyne in the American Revolution, and served in the British West Indies against the Napoleonic armies in Europe. They defended Canada in the War of 1812 and supported the government in the Rebellion of 1837, and the Red River Rebellion. Their tradition of service continues in modern times including both World Wars in which Canada took part.

Charles himself joined the British Army as an ensign and rose to the rank of Lieutenant-Colonel seeing active service in the West Indies, Europe and Canada. The highlight of his military career was a victory over disproportionate odds at Chateauguay in 1813.

A Tradition Grows

The military tradition which was Charles' birthright as a de Salaberry had many highlights. A Baron de Sault fought in the Crusades under Godfrey de Bouillon, who captured Jerusalem in 1099 and was given the title King of Jerusalem.

During the sixteenth century, war was virtually the order of the day in France. The royal family, Valois, was on the brink of extinction, and two rival groups were trying to secure the succession. The Guise family was known as the Catholic party; their opponents were the Bourbons, whose candidate was Henry III, King of Navarre.

The confrontation was long, bitter, and cruel. Atrocities were committed for political expediency. The St. Bartholomew's Day massacre of the Huguenot followers of Henry of Navarre is the best remembered. Henry himself was kept a virtual prisoner at the Valois court for two years. Finally, in 1585, there erupted what is known to history as the War of the Three Henrys (Henry III, King of France; Henry III, King of Navarre; Henry, Duke of Guise).

Two years later at the battle of Coutras the de Salaberry motto was coined. Among the Bourbon officers was a de Salaberry who distinguished himself by killing in one-to-one combat one of the leading Guise warriors. He also wounded but spared the life of a less adept swordsman. Henry of Navarre, who had watched both of these episodes, galloped over and called out,

"Force à Superbe, Mercy à Faible –
voila ta devise, de Salaberry."

Since that time this motto, which can be roughly translated as "Strength against the Mighty, Mercy to the Weak" has been a part of the family's coat of arms.

Other de Salaberrys carried on the military tradition in the infantry, cavalry, and navy; they fought against the Moors, English, Infidels, and Christians.

Having established themselves through their military exploits, the family entered the arena of public affairs. De Salaberrys participated in the councils of state, held public office, and continued the traditions of service to king and country.

Charles-Simon de Salaberry was named Military Governor in the Ardennes in the early eighteenth century; his oldest son was in charge of the Treasury Department for that area; and his nephew Abbé de Salaberry was state councillor in 1736.

18

Into the New World

The first de Salaberry to come to New France (as Canada was known) was Charles' grandfather, Michel. He arrived in 1735 as captain of a merchant vessel planning to stay for a short holiday. His visit turned out to be considerably longer than expected, because he met and on 17 May married Catherine Rouer de Villeroy.

His bride was a widow with five children; in the next five years she had five more. Three of these, Michel, Angelique, and Denise, died while still quite young. Marie Angelique married a wealthy French gentleman, M. Prevost, and moved with him to France. The fifth child, Louise, became a nun at the General Hospital in Quebec and lived to the age of 84. Five years after her marriage, Madame de Salaberry died.

Michel felt the loss of his wife very strongly and sought refuge in danger. He left the merchant service and joined the French navy. In 1745 with the renewal of hostilities with England he volunteered for some of the more dangerous missions, running messages and supplies through the British fleet.

With the fall of the fortress of Louisbourg in June, 1745, the French fleet lost the base from which it protected the Gulf of St. Lawrence. This jeopardized its supply lines to Quebec. In order to relieve the situation in Quebec, Michel volunteered to run two ships through from France to the gulf, winter there and get down to Quebec in the spring. The plan fell through when his partner in the enterprise, Hiriard, had a change of heart and withdrew.

Undeterred, Michel came up with a new plan. He prepared the goelette, *La Marie*, and set sail into the North Atlantic on 16 November. It was a violent, storm-tossed passage; sails were torn, cables parted, and finally the mizzenmast broke. On 6 January 1746, the ship limped into the harbour of St Pierre, in the gulf. The condition of the ship and crew was deplorable, and as soon as they could they sailed for the West Indies to repair the vessel and await the break up of ice in the St Lawrence.

Late in April they sailed from Martinique under escort. After several days at sea, they were spotted by a British warship. While the escort turned to do battle,

D GARVIN

The de Salaberry Manor in Beauport as it appeared when it was used by Montcalm as a Field Headquarters during the Siege of Quebec.

Michel escaped with his supply vessel. He arrived in Quebec on the 6 June, delivered his supplies, and spent the rest of the summer patrolling the gulf.

He was promoted to the rank of Captain in 1748 and two years later he remarried. His wife, Madelaine Louise, was the daughter of one of the leading colonial seigneurs, Ignace Juchereau Duchesnay of St Denis.

A few years after his marriage, Michel purchased from his mother-in-law one of the oldest seigneuries in the colony, Beauport. It had originally been granted to her grandfather, Dr Robert Griffard in 1634. The de Salaberry family now had a firm and respectable base in the New World. The strategic location of the manor house was significant during the ensuing Seven Years' War. In 1759, General Montcalm used it as his headquarters to command the flank against Wolfe.

The Seven Years' War (1756-1763) was the culmination of a long struggle between France and England over colonial territory. Continuing his naval services, Michel spent much of the war on the run between France and Louisbourg, which had been returned to the French in 1748 by the treaty of Aix-la-Chapelle. Finally, when commanding *La Fidèle* in 1758, he was trapped by the English, who called on him to surrender. His answer was:

> *Je commande La Fidèle* – fidèle je reste –
> Salaberry.

He then blew up his ship, made it to shore and, with the help of Indians, escaped.

The following year Quebec fell before the combined operations of Admiral Saunders and General Wolfe. By late the following spring, the reduction of the colony was complete and French power in North America was broken. The Peace of Paris in 1763 finalized the transfer of New France to the English.

The loss of the colony was a bitter pill for the old captain to swallow. Unable to reconcile himself to British rule, he left Beauport in 1766 for his homeland. King Louis XV was not unmindful of the valuable services that de Salaberry had rendered the crown, and soon after his return to France he was summoned to a royal audience

21

The Honourable Louis de Salaberry, Seigneur of Beauport and Charles' father.

where the king presented him with the coveted *Croix de St-Louis*. The following year this honour was augmented by the allowance of 1,000 livres (about $7,000) which helped make his last days a little more comfortable. He died a year later in the port of La Rochelle.

A New Era

The only child of Michel's second marriage was a son, Ignace Michel Louis Antoine (known as Louis). He was born in Beauport on 4 July 1752, and it was to be his destiny to make the family name as respected in British Canada as it had been in New France.

His introduction to violence came early. He was only seven when Wolfe laid siege to Quebec. During the siege, he and his mother took refuge in the General Hospital, where his half-sister was a nun. The hospital lay outside the walls of the city and was considered neutral territory.

Soon after the fall of Quebec it seems that he went to France because the schools in the colony, cut off from their source of financial support, the French crown, had closed and Michel was determined that his son would have a good education. As soon as the Séminaire de Québec was to reopen, Louis returned and on 7 October 1765 he was the first student to register. After four years there he returned to France to complete his studies.

During this second visit Louis made a number of friends among the nobles of France with whom he studied. After his return home, he kept up these friendships through correspondence. Twenty years later when France was shaken by the terrors of the revolution, a number of the nobles who fled sought refuge with their old friend at his peaceful seigneury, Beauport. The litany of guests at the manor house during that period included the Marquis and Marquise de Ste-Aulaire, the Comte de Colbert, the Marquis de Barail, and the Comte Castor de St-Victor.

As soon as possible after the completion of his studies, Louis embarked on a military career. He began that career as a private. It was a good time to enter the service because of the increasing discontent in the Thirteen

23

Colonies. At dawn on 19 April 1775, at Lexington, the first shots of the American Revolution were fired. It was not until the following year that the struggle became a War of Independence when, on Louis' twenty-fourth birthday, 4 July 1776, the Declaration of Independence was signed.

The Americans hoped that they could make Canada a fourteenth colony, and therefore prevent its use as a British base for the invasion of the other thirteen. Accordingly, plans were prepared for the campaign. General Montgomery and his troops were to enter Canada by the Richelieu Valley, take Montreal, and move down the St Lawrence to Quebec. Colonel Benedict Arnold and his force were to enter Canada through Maine, via the Kennebec and Chaudière rivers. The two armies were to meet at Quebec.

The first serious obstacle in Montgomery's path through the Richelieu valley was Fort St-Jean. At the outbreak of hostilities, the fort was secured on 10 June 1775 by a volunteer force of Canadian Seigneurs under M. de Belestre. This is the first recorded action of Canadian militia serving without the support of regular troops during the British regime. Louis de Salaberry was a part of this force that held the fort until Major Charles Preston took over. Preston brought with him 512 British regulars and 20 Royal Highland Emigrants, thereby raising the garrison strength to about 622.

Montgomery opened the siege of Fort St-Jean on 17 September 1775. For 48 days the garrison held out. Below them (between St-Jean and Montreal), Fort Chambly was surrendered disgracefully to an insignificant force of Americans and local sympathizers. The arms, ammunition, and provisions were not destroyed, but rather brought quickly to bolster the besiegers at Fort St-Jean.

The British governor, Sir Guy Carleton, was unable to raise a relieving force in Montreal. The garrison was on its own. Grimly, they hung on, knowing that each day that they could delay the American advance won an extra day for preparing the defence of Quebec.

Finally, on 3 November, Preston signed the Articles of Capitulation. Article 2 stipulated that

> The garrison shall march out with the honors of war.
> This is due to their fortitude and perseverance.

De Salaberry was twice wounded during the siege, and one of these incidents well illustrates the remarkable strength for which he became famous. On 1 November toward the end of the siege, a barrack block collapsed when it received a direct hit. All the occupants had been able to escape the building except Louis, who had been trapped by the falling debris. Quickly his friends started digging through the rubble trying to find his body. What they found was not a corpse but an amazing demonstration of physical strength. When they reached him, he was on his hands and knees on the floor and supporting on his back the upper floor which had fallen in on him. The strain of the tremendous weight had burst almost every blood vessel in his body but he was still very much alive. The men hurriedly shored up the fallen floor and pulled him out, whereupon he resumed his post on the pallisades.

Shortly after the capture of Fort St-Jean Louis was released and returned to active service. In 1777 his unit was attached to General Burgoyne's army of 4,000 British and 3,000 Germans for a large scale offensive. Moving south, they captured Crown Point and Ticonderoga but soon ran into problems. Time was lost building roads through the forests, supplies were running low, foraging parties were unsuccessful and, finally, the army of General Howe which was to join them did not appear. The situation was desperate because barring Burgoyne's way at Saratoga was General Horatio Gates with a Continental army of 12,000 men that was still growing as reinforcements continued to arrive.

"Gentlemen Johnny" Burgoyne tried gallantly to cut through the American army but his losses were too great. When he finally surrendered on 17 October, he had fewer than 3,500 effectives left, less than half the force with which he had begun the campaign. It was largely on the strength of this American victory that France allied herself to the revolutionaries.

Louis de Salaberry received a serious wound in the right knee at Saratoga and although the leg was saved, he was to suffer frequently from its effects. He and the other prisoners resisted entreaties to join the American cause, and were finally released on parole having given their word not to fight again in that war.

While on his parole, Louis courted and, on 18 February 1778 married Francoise Catherine Hertel de Pierreville. The couple settled into life at Beauport and in the course of the next fourteen years they had ten children, three of whom died at birth.

When the war finally ended in 1783, Louis retired on half-pay with the rank of major. On 1 September of the following year he sailed for Paris aboard the *La Madona*. It seems that one of the principle objects of the trip was the gathering of archival material on the family, but Louis also visited his many relatives and friends, was presented to King Louis XVI, and saw the famous Montgolfier brothers undertake a balloon flight. The Comte Victoire de Salaberry, with whom he spent a good deal of time, later became one of the victims of the French Revolution – he was executed in 1794 during the Reign of Terror.

When Louis returned to Quebec he took a more active role in political life. The influx of Loyalists from the United States had brought about agitation for political reform. Louis opposed the constitutional changes that were being mooted and which would, in fact, change the whole nature and character of the country. Petitions, speeches and editorials, could not stop the changes and in 1791 the Constitutional Act was passed dividing Canada into two provinces, Upper Canada (now Ontario) and Lower Canada (now Quebec). Each of these was to have an elected assembly, a dramatic change from the previous system of government by a governor and appointed councillors. The first election in Lower Canada was held in June 1792. Prompted by his friends and aware of the need to participate in the system in order to have an effective voice, Louis campaigned for and won a seat in that first elected assembly.

In 1794 the governor, Sir Guy Carleton, Baron Dorchester, commissioned a new regiment, the Royal Canadian Volunteers to better ensure the security of the country against the fledgling United States. He chose three officers to raise the regiment: Baron Joseph de Longueuil as Colonel, Louis de Salaberry as Major, and Francois Dambourges as Captain. They recruited 600 men and chose as their motto "Try Us". The primary role of the new regiment was garrison duty; it spent two years in each of Montreal, Sorel, and Quebec. It was disbanded in 1801 after Dorchester had returned to England.

Soldiering was only one of Louis' many activities. He was named a Justice of the Peace for the District of Quebec on 2 April 1794. He was a signatory to the address of welcome to the Duke of Kent when the latter arrived in Quebec in August 1791 to command the British garrison and to the farewell address to Baron Dorchester when he left in 1796. On the political scene, he was re-elected to the Assembly in 1804 and 1808, named to the Executive Council in 1808 and to the Legislative Council in 1817. He became Deputy Superintendent of Indians in 1801 and Inspector of Forests in 1808.

Withal, Louis was a man of letters. The manor house at Beauport, with its Norman roof, large windows, and big rooms boasted a fine library reflecting the seigneur's diversified interests ranging from the Latin classics to the practical sciences. As Director of the Agricultural Society of Quebec, he wrote a booklet entitled *Observations sur les défauts de l'agriculture en Canada*, in 1789. He was interested in the theatre and helped in a production of "The Barber of Seville".

When Prince Edward, Duke of Kent was stationed in Quebec (August 1791 – January 1794), he and Louis became good friends, and their friendship endured the vicissitudes of the careers of both men. Many letters passed between them in English, French, and Latin. Edward became the godfather of Louis' youngest son and sponsored careers in the British army for all four of the de Salaberry boys.

Just before the outbreak of war with the United States in 1812, Louis again presented himself for military service. He was named Lt-Colonel of the first battalion of the Select Embodied Militia, but before he could see action his right leg became paralyzed on 25 October 1812 as a result of his old war wound, and he was forced to retire. However, he continued in the political sphere and on 4 December 1817 Lord Sherbrooke named him to the Legislative Council, the closest advisors to the governor. He remained a member of this body until the discussion of the union of Upper and Lower Canada was brought before it in 1822. This union was designed to break the French majority which dominated the Legislature in Lower Canada. Louis refused to be a party to such a plan and resigned his seat in the government. His intransigence cost him the half-pay military pension he had earned long before.

The controversy over the union was a stormy one; committees of leading citizens formed in the major centres to oppose it. Louis was president of the committee in Quebec City and his son Charles was a member of the one in Montreal. The committees collected 60,000 signatures on a petition against the union. These last efforts, however, were too much for Louis. He had been in ill health for several years, and died on 22 March 1828 at the age of 75.

New Loyalties – Old Traditions

Louis had four sons: Charles, Maurice, François, and Edward. Maurice Roch was born in 1783, and as soon as he was old enough he entered the British Army under the patronage of the Duke of Kent. He was sent to the jungles of the East Indies, where he fell victim to an enemy that military science was ill equipped to combat, intestinal fever. At the age of 26 he died of the disease in the East Indian community of Tomboodra. His career had been short, but he had won the respect of all the military personnel with whom he had served. His men and his superior officers raised a monument to him in that distant part of the empire.

François Louis was two years younger than Maurice. Since he bore his father's name, he was usually called Chevalier, a tradition of those days. He too had the misfortune of being posted to the East Indies where, in 1811 he fell victim to the same disease as had Maurice. He died in the vicinity of Secumderabad. Military service was taking a quick and heavy toll of the de Salaberrys.

The youngest son, Edward Alphonse, was born in 1792 and was named for his godfather, H.R.H. Prince Edward,

28

Duke of Kent, and his godmother, Alphonsine de Mongenet de Fortison, baronne de Saint Laurent. He was sent to military school in England and was a frequent guest of the Duke on his vacations from school.

When his education as an artillery officer was completed, Edward was sent to join General Wellington in Spain. One of the prime objectives for the British in the Peninsula was the fortress of Badajoz. Two previous sieges[1] had been unsuccessful, but on 16 March 1812, Wellington himself commanded the investing. The bombardment of the walls lasted until 6 April, when three breaches had been effected. That night, at ten o'clock, an elaborate five-pronged assault was launched – one to each breach and two scaling attempts.

Edward de Salaberry led his men in a desperate charge at one of the breaches. They were repelled with heavy losses. The breaches had been entrenched, mined, and were well defended. Forty separate assaults were made against the breaches that night with phenomenal losses. Eventually Badajoz fell, but so had very many brave men – 4, 924 casualties, of whom 378 were officers.[2]

The twisted body of young de Salaberry was found where he had fallen at the mouth of the breach. He was the only one of Louis' sons to die in battle. Near him lay his comrade-in-arms, Francis Simcoe, son of John Graves Simcoe, Upper Canada's first governor. He also had been a protégé of the Duke of Kent. It is said that this is the first time that Wellington ever wept over the extent of a casualty list; he did it only once again, at Waterloo.

Chapter Two

Lessons in the Indies

From Infancy to Infantry

During his childhood Charles de Salaberry gave little indication of the strength and determination that would characterize his active military career. He was born in the manor house at Beauport on 19 November 1778, and was such a sickly infant that his parents feared for his life. They immediately called in a priest to conditionally baptize the child. The haste with which this was done is indicated by the fact that Canon Charles-Regis Rigauville, the Vicar-General of the Quebec Diocese, who performed the baptism, also stood in as godfather. Happily for history, the boy survived both his birth and six months of frequent colic. By the age of nine months he was taking his first steps.

Little is known of Charles' early years. But we do know that as soon as he possibly could he followed in the family's military tradition: at the age of 14, he enlisted as a gentleman volunteer in the 44th Regiment of Foot. Sponsored, as were his brothers, by the Duke of Kent, Charles obtained a commission as Ensign in the 60th Regiment of Foot (The Royal Americans) on 10 April 1793.

At that time the 60th Regiment had two battalions stationed in Canada and two in the West Indies; it was to one of the latter that de Salaberry was sent to learn the art of soldiering. Carrying a letter of introduction to Captain Fortier and about two guineas in cash he sailed for Martinique. On his arrival he was immediately posted to the island of St Vincent where he joined his regiment and began his active military career on 28 July 1794.

31

Political Pawns

A military posting to the West Indies was no sinecure. As producers of sugar the islands were of vital economic importance to both France and England but were, at the same time, difficult and expensive to protect. As a result, whenever the mother countries were at war, which was frequently, there would be a great deal of scrambling for these jewels in the Caribbean. In addition to formal warfare there were frequent and bloody slave revolts and the scourge of tropical diseases to contend with.

The islands had changed hands several times through both the fortunes of war and purchases of peace. During the Seven Years' War the British Navy captured Guadaloupe, Martinique, Grenada, St Vincent, and St Lucia. That war ended in 1763 with the Peace of Paris in which France ceded to Britain not only Canada but also Grenada, St Vincent, Dominica (San Domingo), and Tobago. France's alliance with the rebelling American colonies won back for her the islands of St Lucia and Tobago at the Treaty of Paris in 1783.

The hostilities in which de Salaberry was to play a part were a direct result of the execution of Louis XVI in 1793. Britain reacted to this regicide by expelling the French diplomatic representative. France replied by declaring war. Britain quickly organized a coalition with Prussia, Austria, Spain, Sardinia, and Piedmont and subsidized them in the bulk of the fighting on the continent while she, with the mobility provided by her powerful navy, moved to strike a decisive blow in the French West Indies.

Baptism of Fire

The principal theatre of operations at the time of de Salaberry's arrival in the West Indies in late July 1794 was the island of Guadaloupe. The island resembles a figure eight about 50 kilometres long and 40 kilometres wide, lying on a northeast-southwest axis and is divided at the centre by the canal-like Salée. The northern section is known as Grande-Terre and the southern as Basse-Terre. It had been taken by English forces in April of the previous

32

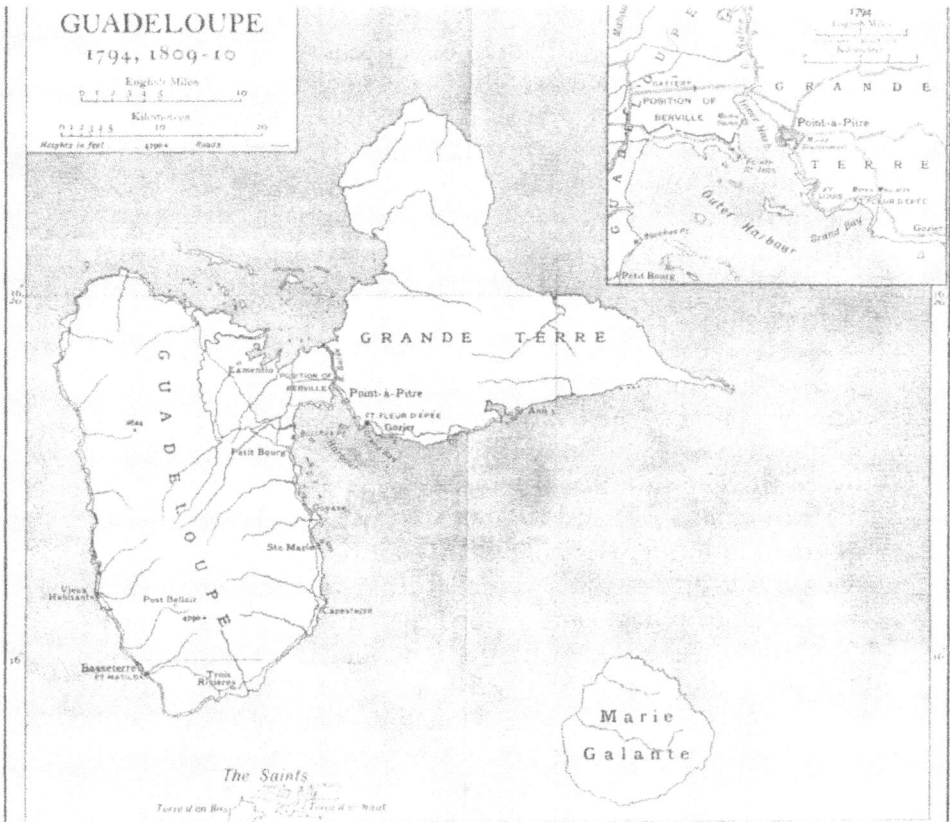

Guadaloupe during de Salaberry's first campaign.

year, but the French had returned in strength and by the end of June had regained control of Grande-Terre. The British general, Sir Charles Grey, sent for reinforcements from St Lucia, St Vincent, and Antigua. Ensign de Salaberry was among the troops that boarded the ship *Veteran* and sailed for Basse-Terre in Guadaloupe.

Every effort was made to drive the French from Grande-Terre. In a series of encounters, many of them with bayonets,[1] the British drove back their enemy and eventually contained them in Fort Fleur d'Espée. The fort itself was stoutly defended by the French republican general Victor Hugues, whose mass executions earned him the nickname "Robespierre of the Isles". He held out against repeated assaults until the rainy season began. The sickness and fever that came with this season struck the British forces very hard, and so reduced their fighting strength that they had to retire across the Salée to Basse-Terre.

Here they attempted to consolidate their hold by strengthening their camp on the isthmus that separated the two parts of the island. However, the strength of that position was somewhat illusory as many of the troops were ill. The number of effectives in de Salaberry's own battalion was reduced to about 200, although he himself seemed immune. His good health signalled him out for a variety of duties that would ordinarily have gone to a more senior officer, and helped him to win an early promotion to the rank of Lieutenant and the command of the grenadier company (25 August 1794) at the age of 15.

In late September the French took the offensive and launched a two-pronged attack by sea. One force landed south of the Salée at Gayavé and the other, north of it at Lamentin. They marched inland to join forces and effectively encircled the British camp at the Salée. On 6 October the camp fell after a week of siege, and the French, 2,000 strong, headed for the town of Basse-Terre, destroying the homes of planters en route.

On 16 October General Prescott, in command at Basse-Terre, destroyed all the batteries of the town and retired to Fort Matilda with his 600 men. De Salaberry commanded the grenadier company during the ensuing siege. The shortage of officers meant that each one had to perform

34

extra duty, and Charles was often on guard duty for two days and nights at a stretch.

On 6 December he was on guard duty upon a section of the ramparts that was under extremely heavy fire. Five hundred shots and 50 shells were shot at them in five hours, and the number of killed and wounded rose steadily. The grenadier company of the 4th Battalion, which he was commanding, was one of the hardest hit – but worse was yet to come. Day after day the French kept up the pressure until Prescott, faced with an alarming casualty rate and crumbling defences, ordered an evacuation on 10 December. De Salaberry's company covered the retreat. It was only through dint of his own example that the sixteen-year-old lieutenant was able to maintain discipline throughout the sanguinary battle. When the company was paraded after the evacuation, it was found that only three men, including de Salaberry, had not been wounded in the ordeal.

It was quite an introduction to soldiering but it left him undaunted and, if anything, it seemed to whet his appetite. In his letters home – perhaps not wanting to worry his parents – he made light of the affair and claimed that he had his grandfather's good luck.

Finances were actually more of a concern for de Salaberry than the dangers of battle. His uniform alone cost him close to forty pounds and the cost of everything was about three times what it was at home. The pay of a junior officer was barely enough to cover the necessities. Messing cost $3.00 per month plus rations, and laundry was $4.00 per month. He could not even afford to drink wine. But he assured his father that he would not run into debt and he made good his promise. The only way to improve his financial situation was to obtain a promotion, but for the third lieutenant of a battalion, captaincies were hard to come by.

Swordsmanship was also an important aspect of his life. De Salaberry was quite concerned that being with a light company he was never in one place long enough to engage the services of a fencing master. As we shall soon see, the art of fencing was not one to be neglected.

The winter of 1795 saw much military activity. In January the French reinforced Guadaloupe with about

6,000 men. There was an insurrection on Grenada in early March. The Caribs revolted on St Vincent in the same month. Trouble spread to St Lucia in April. Throughout most of this activity, de Salaberry was confined by a bad case of tropical fever at Prince Rupert's Head, Dominica and it was not until June that he was able to resume active service.

His recovery was timely because the French landed on the north-east coast of Dominica, at Paqoua Bay, in that same month. In a swift campaign the British and the local militia crossed the island and, after some initial fighting, outmanouvered the French, surrounded and captured them. By the twenty-seventh the situation was restored to normal. There were two further French attempts at establishing a beachhead, but both were easily repulsed.

The British determined to move against Martinique. This island had the finest harbour in the Eastern Caribbean, and so it constituted a high priority objective. The campaign was under the command of General Sir Charles Grey and Admiral Sir John Jervis. The Royal Americans, now down to about 200 effectives, was assigned to the expedition and de Salaberry again led his grenadier company into action. According to the reports the British victory on Martinique was gained without the loss of a single life. The island was retained by Britain until 1801 when it was returned to France in exchange for Trinidad.

In an effort to expedite de Salaberry's promotion, the Duke of Kent requested his transfer to his own regiment, the 7th. Before that transfer could be effected, however, the policy of seniority in the British army was changed. Up to that time promotion within a battalion had been based on seniority within that battalion. Now the regiment was made the basis and de Salaberry would become junior lieutenant in a regiment with four battalions. Immediately on learning this news, Kent refused the transfer in de Salaberry's name and wrote to the Commander-in-Chief, West Indies, Lt-Gen. Sir Ralph Abercromby, requesting a captaincy for de Salaberry. Before that letter arrived, the notice of the transfer was published in the official government Gazette and Abercromby therefore ordered de Salaberry to sail to Halifax to join the 7th.

The voyage to Halifax took seventeen days and de Salaberry arrived on 1 July 1796. His position was now a little unclear so Kent kept him there pending further developments. During this stay in Halifax he was a house guest of Mr Hayman, a family friend who had in his turn been entertained at Beauport.

By the end of July there was still no decision on de Salaberry's position, so Kent sent him home for a holiday. He sailed on the frigate *Pearl* which was taking Captain Hunter's company of the 4th regiment to Quebec. Although he had been away only for two years, his reception at home would have done a hero proud. Word of his experiences in the West Indies had preceded him, and friends came from miles away to visit and join in the parties and dancing.

De Salaberry enjoyed that summer at home. In September he received word that Kent had been successful in getting him reinstated in the 4th battalion of the 60th with the same status as before. The holiday over, he packed his bags and boarded the *Earl of Moira* at Quebec for the trip to Halifax.

As the ship cleared the river and sailed into the Gulf of St Lawrence, the weather deteriorated and the ship was soon in a terrific storm. It was blown off course and despite the efforts of the captain and crew, it ploughed into the rocks off Ile St Jean.[2] Fortunately, not a single person was lost in the accident, but it was not until 25 October that de Salaberry finally reported for duty in Halifax.

By this time there was talk of reorganizing the 60th regiment; Kent kept de Salaberry until that sorted itself out. Much of his time in Halifax was spent on recruiting duties, at which he turned out to be quite successful.

The Duke of Kent was very active in Freemasonry in Canada, and, in fact, radically reorganized it. De Salaberry, himself, was received as a Master Mason on 2 February 1797 in Military Lodge Red Rose #2.

The cost of living in Halifax was high. In order to help de Salaberry financially, Kent had him seconded to the ship *Asia*. Spain had just allied herself to France and de Salaberry, with thirty men, joined the vessel on a mission to harrass Spanish shipping. The *Asia* sailed from Halifax in early February and returned on 20 June after an unspectacular voyage.

Soon after his return de Salaberry received orders to rejoin his regiment in the West Indies. He sailed from Halifax on 3 July 1797 bound for Martinique. When he arrived there at the end of the month, he found that his battalion had left the day before for its new posting in Jamaica. He followed and rejoined it there. Two more years of active service in the West Indies won him at long last a promotion to Captain on 10 July 1799.

Toward the end of that year troubles broke out anew in Jamaica and martial law was declared. Lt-Col Ainsley, the Commanding Officer of the 4th battalion, was named Major-General of Militia and he took de Salaberry as his aide-de-camp and Brigade Major. Ainsley recommended him very highly for his conduct during that tour of duty.

The 60th (Royal Americans) Regiment of Foot was a particularly interesting unit. It had originally been raised at New York and Philadelphia in 1775 as a combined Colonial Corps and Foreign Legion. A special Act of the British Parliament authorized the granting of commissions to foreigners "to serve in the Americas only". Their uniform was scarlet with dark blue facings and silver (for the officers) lace with two blue stripes. There were four battalions, each with a grenadier company.

The 60th had played a prominent part in the capture of Canada. During the attack on Quebec in 1759, General Wolfe was so impressed with their fighting at Montmorency Falls that he gave them their regimental motto: *Celer et Audax* — Swift and Bold. In 1797, the year de Salaberry rejoined it, the regimental march was changed from "The British Grenadier" to the "Duke of York's March" in honour of their new Colonel-in-Chief, and the Maltese Cross was adopted as the regimental badge. At the end of the nineteenth century (when it was known as the King's Royal Rifle Corps) it displayed more battle honours (33) than any other regiment in the Service.

De Salaberry's fellow officers were therefore professional soldiers drawn from many nations; England, Prussia, Switzerland, Hanover and many others. Among them all there was only one other French Canadian, a young officer named des Rivières. Like de Salaberry, he was a protégé of the Duke of Kent.

With such a cross section of nationalities it was inevitable that difficulties should arise, and the maintenance of peaceful relations in the mess was not an easy job. The Germans, especially, were accomplished swordsmen and they enjoyed crossing swords with their fellow officers as much as with the enemy.

One evening des Rivières was lured into a duel by one of these swordsmen and killed in a very unequal struggle. At breakfast next morning, the duellist snidely remarked that he had just "despatched a French Canadian to meet his Maker."[3] De Salaberry, his sense of honour outraged, leapt to his feet but regained sufficient control of himself to answer the braggart with: "We will finish breakfast and then you will have the pleasure of despatching another." This was a reckless challenge because he was still a rank novice with a sword.

In uneasy silence the messmates returned to their meal. De Salaberry had won the admiration and respect of most of his fellow officers, especially the younger ones, and now they cast quick worried looks in his direction. Breakfast over, he deliberately got up and, turning on his heel, strode to the duelling area followed by his supporters. A few minutes later they were joined by the Prussian and his supporters.

De Salaberry took off his tunic and tossed it to a friend. Quietly he took the scabbard from his belt, drew out the sabre, and handed the scabbard to another supporter. With a flourish, the duel began. The older man carefully, but expertly, toyed with his foe, thinking to have a little fun before the kill. De Salaberry kept up a methodical series of attacks as he tried to find his opponent's weak spot and test his reflexes. The man had every reason to be confident; if there was a weakness in his defence de Salaberry could not find it.

Then the fight became more serious, a savage contest with each man's life in the balance. The Prussian's greater experience soon began to assert itself. He parried a weak lunge of the French Canadian and countered with a riposte that scored a terrible gash across the left temple.

39

Blood gushed out blinding de Salaberry as his friends dragged him from the fight.

But de Salaberry wouldn't quit. With a handkerchief binding his wound, he returned to the fight with renewed vigor. No quarter was asked and none was given. What he lacked in experience, he amply made up for in spirit, enthusiasm, and courage – a trio of qualities that turned the tide of battle – and the veteran of many duels found himself more and more on the defensive as de Salaberry pressed his attacks with increasing strength and energy. While de Salaberry was gaining in stride, his older opponent began to tire. Summoning every ounce of energy he could muster, he laid into his opponent with a veritable barrage of attacks, never letting him have a second to return to the offensive. He feigned an attack at the right shoulder, then he switched to a tremendous swipe at the left waist before his tired opponent had completed his first parry, and it was all over. Legend has it that the Prussian's body was sliced in two by that last stroke.[4]

De Salaberry's honour was avenged and was never again challenged. Subsequent to this affair, Colonel Devoe of the 60th regiment reported to the Duke of Kent regarding the young officer:

> He is a young man of distinguished bravery and he will make an excellent officer because he has a dedication to honour engraved in his soul.[5]

Chapter Three

Service in England

A Happy Voyage

Captain Charles de Salaberry took his last look at the West Indies as he sailed north in December 1804. He was heading for his first home leave in seven years. It was an extended furlough of six months, and the climate and home cooking did wonders for his constitution. When it was over, his orders took him to England.

This trip was made more pleasant because he sailed with his brothers Maurice and François Louis (Chevalier) who were also going to join their regiment in England. When they arrived at Gravesend after 56 days at sea, the three of them, in fine spirits, walked the 35 or so kilometres to London.

Several battalions of the 60th were now in England. An act had been passed in 1804 permitting up to 10,000 foreign troops to serve in the country and, in fact, the 60th was expanded by several battalions.

Service in England had a number of compensations for de Salaberry. He was able to meet his brothers from time to time and had frequent opportunities to visit his patron the Duke of Kent and Mme de St Laurent at both Kensington Palace and their summer house, Castle Lodge. Furthermore, he was in a better position to know what[1] postings were available and to apply for them quickly. His goal was a posting to his homeland so that he could settle down.

He was at Kensington Palace when word was received that General Burton was going to be offered the command in Canada. This was exciting news because if Burton, who was a good friend of Kent, went he would certainly take de Salaberry with him. All the plans were made for this move. He even arranged a special leave

41

Lt. Gen. Francis Baron de Rottenburg, K.C.H.

with his two brothers before they left on a posting to Ireland. He thought he would be gone by the time they returned. The whole thing fell through when Burton refused the command in Canada.

Recruiting for the King

Disappointed, de Salaberry threw himself into his new assignment. He was posted to the 5th Battalion of the 60th under Lieutenant Colonel Baron de Rottenburg and was put in charge of recruiting. This unit was the first green-coated rifle battalion in the army.

De Rottenburg was born in Austria but was a naturalized British subject who had raised the 5th Battalion at Cowes, Isle of Wight, in December 1797. Originally it was composed of 400 men of Hompesch's Mounted Riflemen and 500 of Lowenstein's Chasseurs. It was organized on the Austrian model as a special corps of Jägers or Riflemen. Their green uniforms with red facings and the muzzle-loading rifles (likely the ten and a half pound Baker rifle) were serious breaks with British army tradition. The Battalion was the beginning of a new system for the army.

The changes went even further. De Rottenburg wrote *Regulations for the Exercise of Riflemen and Light Infantry and Instructions for Their Conduct in the Field*, which was published in 1798 and became a very influential textbook. Among the changes in drill advocated by de Rottenburg were a free, natural rhythm in marching to replace the staccato style that was slower and more tiring. In fact, the usual marching pace for his Riflemen was 140 paces to the minute (compared to the infantry standard of 120) and many movements were done on the double. Quick, silent drill, shorter commands, and the carrying of the rifle at the trail rather than the slope were other innovations. He also introduced "manoeuvre by bugle call". His grasp of de Rottenburg's techniques was manifest when de Salaberry later undertook the training of the Canadian Voltigeurs.

De Salaberry's recruiting experience in Halifax served him well as he travelled about England enlisting men for both de Rottenburg and Kent. One of the techniques he used was to re-enlist men from other regiments that were being disbanded or whose term of service was completed. There was serious competition among recruiting officers from the various regiments for these eligible, already trained soldiers. Evidence of his success can be found in the numerous letters of congratulation from Kent. His success, however, antagonized others, most particularly General Sir George Prevost who felt that de Salaberry was hiring good men away from him. This was an unfortunate *contretemps* in view of the fact that Prevost was to play a prominent role in Canada during the next war with the United States.

During the summer of 1806 young Edward de Salaberry was expected to arrive in England to begin his formal military education. At the end of August, de Salaberry heard that a frigate was due in at Portsmouth from Quebec. He and Maurice hurried to the port city. While searching the harbour, they met Captain Bramley of the frigate and asked if he had a passenger from Quebec. Bramley said no and the disappointed and worried brothers then asked if he had not seen M. de Salaberry in Quebec. This brought a more favorable response and Bramley replied that certainly he had seen M. de Salaberry and that, moreover, he had his son on board and was expecting him ashore in a few minutes. Somehow Edward had known the Captain and so was not considered a passenger; but it had given the brothers a few bad moments.

The three brothers left Portsmouth for the nearby city of Gosport, an important supply depot where de Salaberry was stationed on his recruiting duties. Their arrival there was the occasion for a great family reunion. The four de Salaberry boys and their cousins, Chevalier and Juchereau Duchesnay, were all together and celebrations went far into the night.

The fine hand of the Duke of Kent was responsible for this reunion. Knowing that Edward was due to arrive in late summer, he recalled Maurice and Chevalier from Ireland and sent them to help Charles with his recruiting in Gosport. They arrived there in the middle of July and soon after the reunion they were returned to their units.

Early in 1807 Kent's 2nd Battalion was ordered to the East Indies and Maurice and Chevalier met with their older brother on the eve of their departure. Remembering his earlier experiences, Charles gave each of them some pocket money, and to Chevalier he also gave his watch.

Kent continued his efforts on de Salaberry's behalf and tried unsuccessfully to get him appointed A.D.C. first to Sir Charles Green on Malta, then to Sir James Craig who was going to Canada. He even applied for a posting with Sir James Cockburn in Curaçao, which reportedly had the healthiest climate in the West Indies.

Romantic Interlude

The 5th Battalion of the 60th was sent to Ireland in September 1807 to perform garrison duty near Cork.

De Salaberry had an aunt living in Cork, his mother's sister who had married a Fortesque. The Fortesques were an old Norman family who had come to Britain with William the Conqueror and fought at the Battle of Hastings in 1066. De Salaberry's interest in the family, however, was focused on his cousin, Maria Fortesque. She was 22 years old with dark hair and eyes, and was as interested in him as he was in her. Whenever he could get leave he would head straight for her family's house; and it wasn't long before the two of them were thinking and planning for a future together.

De Salaberry wrote to his friend and confidante Mme de St Laurent to tell her of his love and his plans to marry Maria. The reaction of Kent and Mme de St Laurent was sympathetic but shattering. In a very carefully worded letter Kent pointed out what the young lovers had not considered: their likely future on his soldier's pay. It was a dismal prospect; living in barracks, unable to afford the simplest little luxuries, penny-pinching all the time. In his brutally frank assessment, Kent pointed out that:

> if under any circumstances, it can be right for you to think of it (marriage), it would be if chance threw in your way, a woman of respectable character,

45

who is enabled to give you, the day you marry her,
that independence which there is little prospect of
your ever being able to give her . . . .[2]

De Salaberry was shaken, but he knew that Kent
was speaking from the heart and furthermore, that he
was right. There was no way that he could subject Maria
to the kind of life he could provide. He wrote to his aunt
to call off their engagement, and included a copy of Kent's
letter to help explain his position. In his own files, he
endorsed Kent's letter as:

Advice to me on the subject of marrying – paying
me a handsome compliment as a soldier.

Back to War

Charles found enough work to prevent himself from
dwelling on the injustices of the world. De Rottenburg
was promoted to Major General. De Salaberry received
his long awaited promotion to Major and was appointed
aide-de-camp to de Rottenburg. And large scale military
action was in the offing.

In a bid to reduce the Napoleonic threat, a campaign
was being planned for the capture of Walcheren Island,
at the mouth of the Scheldt river. It was a Dutch island
but under the control of the French. The island had strategic significance in that it controlled the Scheldt estuary,
but the campaign's real objective was to create a diversion
in favor of the allied land forces.

The Earl of Chatham, a parade square general, was
placed in command of the land forces which included over
25,000 men. The naval force of 84 vessels of war was commanded by Vice-Admiral Sir Richard Strachan. This was
an impressive force, but it was dogged by troubles from
the start. Political interference and inter-service rivalry
and friction were rampant; and the men had serious doubts
about the quality of leadership.

The force was divided into three wings or fleets. The
North Fleet with 34 vessels under Admiral Sir Richard
Keats carried Sir John Hope and his 8,000 men. Their

The Scheldt Estuary 1809

SCHOUWEN

Zierikzee

Steen Deep

Roompot

East Scheldt

Breesand

Haak

East Kapelle

NORTH BEVELAND

Domburg

Veere

West Kapelle

WALCHEREN

Zoutelande

Middleburg

Kattendijke

Goes

Wemelunge

Kapelle

W. Souburg

E. Souburg

Sloe

SOUTH BEVELAND

Biezlinge

Hansweart

Nolle

Duerloo Channel

Flushing

Borsselen

ANTWERP

Ellewoutsdijk

Wielingen Channel

Breskens

CADZAND

Terneuzen

Blankenburg

N

Sluys

Sandbanks
(dry at low water)

0   5   10   15   20 km

APPROX. SCALE

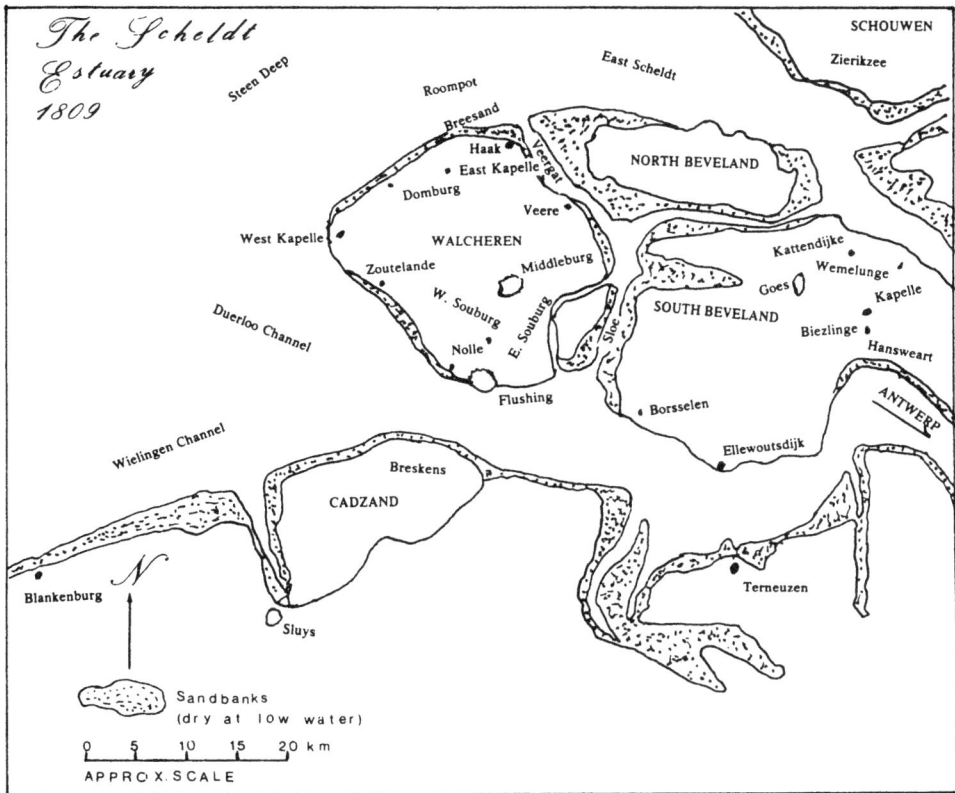

Scene of the ill-fated Walcheren Expedition, 1809.

47

objective was Shouwen Island to the north of Walcheren. The southern and smallest fleet had 13 vessels under Commodore Owen and 5,000 men under Lord Huntley. Their role was to cover the southern flank of Walcheren by taking Cadzand. The centre and largest fleet with 37 vessels and 12,000 men under Admiral Otway and Sir Eyre Coote was to take Walcheren itself.

After several months of politically caused delays, the fleets finally cleared the English coast on 28 July 1809. After crossing the North Sea, they were opposite Bree-zand and heading south in the very early hours of the morning of 30 July. By 5:30 p.m. de Salaberry was leading his men as they stormed ashore with the left wing of the first wave of troops. The British navy did its job well with covering fire from the ships, and after a short engagement on the beaches the British were able to drive back the French General Osten and his 1,500 men.

De Rottenburg now directed the men to their first objective, Fort Den Haak. Keeping under close cover, they circled around to the rear of the fort. The Dutch commander, General Bruce was unwilling to sacrifice his men for the fleeing French and so abandoned the fort to the English. Chatham established his General Headquarters in the fort while elements of his force were still in the landing process.

The town of Flushing on the south coast had the strongest defences. Therefore the British set out to establish control of the rest of the island in a series of very quick moves so that their flanks would be secure while they concentrated on the strongest target. Moving inland to the centre of the island the British accepted the surrender of Middelburg at dawn the following day, 31 July, and by 8:00 a.m. were investing the coastal town of Veere, six kilometres to the north.

The defence at Veere was the stiffest they had encountered so far, and the fighting went on for 20 hours. De Salaberry was placed in command of the centre, and led repeated charges until the town finally surrendered at 4.00 a.m. on 1 August.

The main body of troops was now divided into three columns. They moved south to Flushing by different routes cleaning out any pockets of resistance as they went. De

Salaberry's main target that day was the town of Koudekirke, southwest of Middelburg. He dispersed the defenders and continued southward. By evening the three columns met near Flushing. They had lost about 300 men.

The principal defence for Flushing was a series of bastions around the town, but most of the strongest guns were on the seaward side which had been assumed to be the source of greatest danger. The French force of about 5,000 men was under the command of General Monnet.

The British erected their siegeworks and began the reduction of the town. De Salaberry commanded the advanced posts throughout the siege. By 10 August the French had lost about 1,500 men and were hemmed in with no hope of reinforcements. On orders from Napoleon, Monnet tried to spring the dikes and flood the entire island, but fortunately this met with little success.

The following day a few British frigates moved in through the passes of Deurloo on the west and Sloe on the east of the town and began a bombardment. They were followed the next day by men-of-war and after a day of bombardment by sea and by land, Chatham made an offer of surrender. It was refused and the British laid on a twenty-four-hour bombardment that knocked out most of the enemy batteries.

On the fourteenth Chatham called for a breather and renewed the offer of surrender. He did not even receive an answer, so he ordered a devastating resumption of fire until Monnet had to sue for surrender on the sixteenth. Walcheren was taken.

De Rottenburg was so impressed with de Salaberry as a fighting officer that he nicknamed him "mon cher marquis de la poudre a canon". De Salaberry, himself was happy to be able to send a souvenir of the campaign to his father: a sword that had been given him as a token of surrender by a French commander.

Chatham had hoped to exploit his success by moving up the Scheldt and taking Antwerp, but the losses he had suffered and the outbreak of a terrible fever killed those hopes. Leaving a force including de Salaberry as a garrison at Flushing, he began to re-embark the remnants of his army on 1 September.

The garrison began falling victim to "Walcheren Fever" and soon half of them were down with it. De Salaberry contacted it and with the other victims he was evacuated to England. A few months later the remnants of the garrison, in desperation, destroyed what was left of the standing fortifications and withdrew from the island.

The Earl of Chatham was made the scapegoat for the affair and was forced to resign his post. The press referred to the Walcheren expedition as "unfortunate", but the soldiers were the victims of political intrigue rather than of the fortunes or misfortunes of war. Not even proper food or medical supplies had been provided for the men.

Concerning the expedition and the role of the army high command, the Duke of Kent wrote, on 25 September 1809:

> It would really seem as if those fellows (for I have no patience to call them anything else) were paid by the enemy to do everything against our troops instead of being supported at a heavy expense by our own government, to provide for their wants.[3]

Fortunately for de Salaberry, he had been in very good shape before the expedition and so the fever was not fatal. Kent invited him to his home to recuperate, but the effects of the fever were to plague him for the rest of his life.

Actually Kensington Palace, near Hyde Park in London, was an ideal place to recuperate. It had originally been built about 1605 and was acquired by William and Mary in 1689 because of its healthy location compared to the other royal residences. King William suffered from asthma and wanted to keep away from dampness. Sir Christopher Wren enlarged it for the royal couple and it was further modified for King George I who designed the still-famous Kensington Gardens. The Serpentine was added by Queen Caroline. George III, Kent's father, chose to live at Buckingham and Windsor so he gave the two lower floors of the main building of Kensington to Kent as his living quarters. Here and in the gardens de Salaberry worked at recruiting his strength.

As the ill-fated year drew to a close, de Salaberry spent Christmas with his youngest brother, Edward, and the Duke of Kent. This was the last time the brothers were to meet. Edward soon sailed for Spain and two years later died at the costly but successful siege of Badajoz.

Chapter Four

Return to Canada

An Uneasy Homeland

De Salaberry's dream of returning to Canada was finally realized when de Rottenburg was posted there shortly after the Walcheren expedition. He landed at Quebec on 19 April 1810, and brought de Salaberry with him as his A.D.C.

The situation at home was a political nightmare. Representative government had been suspended. Newspaper editors were in jail for criticizing the governor, and relations between the English and French speaking citizens had deteriorated badly.

The key issue that had precipitated this situation was that of taxation. The merchants and entrepreneurs, who were primarily English speaking and who dominated the Executive Council, wanted taxation to be based on land. The land owners, who were primarily French speaking and who held the majority in the Legislative Assembly, wanted taxation to be based on imports. The man who should have handled this entirely predictable difference of opinion was the governor, Sir James Craig.

Craig could not see the conflict as an economic one, but interpreted it as racial. On the advice of the English extremists, he "solved" the problem by dissolving the Assembly on 15 May 1809 and calling an election. When the new Assembly shared the views of its predecessor, Craig, thoroughly alarmed now, dissolved it in late February 1810, and dismissed a number of French Canadians from government and militia positions. When the newspaper, *Le Canadien* decried these tactics, the editors and printer were thrown in jail. One of the victims of Craig's policy was Charles' father, Louis who lost both his pension and government position.

Private, Canadian Voltigeurs, (1812-13), from a modern watercolor by G.A. Embleton.

Craig was recalled on 19 June 1811 and replaced as governor by Sir George Prevost, who set about to conciliate the population and consolidate the colony. He moved vigorously ahead with these policies because he was seriously concerned about the defence of the colony.

Relations between Britain and the United States had seriously deteriorated in recent years. The Americans were upset because of the British blockade of Europe during the Napoleonic wars and because ships of the British navy often detained American ships in order to search for deserters. Furthermore, the expansionist policies of President Madison and his group of "War Hawks" seemed to make inevitable a war between the States and the Canadas. In addition, British agents were apparently inciting Indians against settlers in the land west of the States.

When the Americans seemed on the verge of attacking the British colonies to the north, it seemed they would have little difficulty. Upper Canada had about 1,500 Regulars with which to defend a 1,600-kilometre border. In Lower Canada, there were five British battalions of the line (about 4,500 men) while other Regulars were stationed in the Maritimes. Each colony could also muster its militia and a number of Indians; the latter's psychological effect on the enemy was often an important factor in an otherwise indecisive battle. But communications in the Canadas were very poor. Such roads as did exist were in a terrible state, for the most part, and the movement of troops was thereby seriously hampered.

Enter the Voltigeurs

In this situation the governor, Sir George Prevost, was at the end of his tether. He absolutely needed an assurance that the French Canadians would remain loyal, but knew that they had a good many reasons to want to end British rule. Several of Prevost's predecessors had done little to reconcile the *Canadiens* to British rule, and at this critical stage their defection could spell disaster. He looked about for a man around whom the people could rise to the defence of the colony. He decided on the recently returned Charles de Salaberry. It was a wise and logical choice, as history was soon to prove.

Charles was now in his early thirties, a man who could command attention, respect, and, if need be, fear. He was a big man – a little above average height, broad shouldered, strong and stern; he had a reputation as a strict but just officer and a brave and daring soldier. He had just returned home after having spent half his life on the battlefields of the world. He was, in short, a man to whom his countrymen could look with confidence and respect and of whom the government could expect first-class service.

One of his countrymen, Senator L.O. David, describes him as:

> un magnifique ensemble de force, de distinction, de vigeur et de beauté, une puissante organisation debordant de vie et de sève.[1]

Prevost gave de Salaberry the militia rank of Lt-Colonel on 1 April 1812. Two weeks later he signed the orders for the formation of a corps of light infantry to be called the Canadian Voltigeurs and to be organized and commanded by de Salaberry.

In his desperation to increase the number of French Canadians under arms, Governor Prevost promised that he would try to get de Salaberry's Lt-Colonelcy pushed through in the regular army where it had more meaning and remuneration than it did in the militia, providing that de Salaberry recruit more and more men. The minimum strength of the Voltigeurs was raised first to 380 and finally to over 500. The promotion finally came through on 24 September 1812, giving Charles the post of Commandant and Superintendant of the Corps of Canadian Voltigeurs, with the rank of Lt-Colonel in the army. This was an impressive position for a 34-year-old French Canadian to hold in the British Army.

The Voltigeurs were to be armed with light infantry muskets with black accoutrements and a knife. Their uniform was to be grey trousers and hooded tunic, with black cuffs and buttons, red sash, crossbelts, Canadian short boots and light bearskin caps. Their drill comprised simple infantry manoeuvres with an emphasis on sharp-shooting.

De Salaberry's method of recruiting was quite common at the time. He would appoint certain officers on the understanding that they would not receive their commission until they had enlisted a specific quota of men. To qualify as a private in the Voltigeurs one had simply to be between the ages of 17 and 35 and stand no less than 5′3″ (160 CM) in height. These qualifications were certainly not particularly burdensome, and recruiting went on so briskly that the *Quebec Gazette*, reporting near the end of April 1812 recorded:

> The corps now forming under the command of Major de Salaberry is completing with a dispatch worthy of the ancient warlike spirit of the country. Captain Perrault's company was filled up in forty-eight hours, and was yesterday passed by His Excellency the Governor, and the companies of Captains Duchesnay, Panet and L'Ecuyer have now nearly their complement. The young men move in solid columns towards the enlisting officers with an expression of countenance not to be mistaken. The Canadians are awakening from the repose of an age secured to them by good government and virtuous habits. Their anger is fresh – The object of their preparation is simple and distinct. They are to defend their king, known to them only by acts of kindness, and a native country long since made sacred by the exploits of their forefathers.

This may have been a slightly overzealous statement of the case, but it demonstrates a prevalent mood. Fighting men were being drawn from all quarters, and by 6 October 1812, 200 men from the little villages of Blairfindrie, Saint Constant, and Saint Philippe had been gathered for arms drill. The story was the same throughout this area. The corps was quickly completed and put into basic training. They were to see action within the year.

Madame de Salaberry.

A Happier Romance

Despite the political and military challenges that de Salaberry faced on his return, he found time to revive old acquaintances, to visit with relatives, and to live his own life.

He frequently visited and attended parties at the Rouville manor where he met the seigneur's daughter, a dark-haired woman with flashing eyes, Marie-Anne-Julie. De Salaberry was strongly attracted to her and she to him; and a romance was soon flourishing.

There were not the problems there had been with Maria Fortesque. Marie-Anne's father, Jean-Baptiste Melchior Hertel de Rouville, was related to Charles' mother (who was also a member of the widespread Hertel family). He was also an old friend of Charles' father; they had served together in the army and had both taken part in the siege of Fort St-Jean. He was a rich man whose estates included the seigneuries of Rouville, Chambly, Saint-Olivier and others. His manor house on the shore of the Richelieu river at the foot of Mont Saint-Hilaire was an impressive structure.

Marie-Anne and Charles were married on 14 May 1812. As her dowry she brought him the seigneurie of Chambly where the couple were to make their home.

The two fathers-in-law kept up a steady correspondence and de Rouville, who was closer to the actual theatre of war in which the young de Salaberry was active, kept Louis up to date on the progress of the fighting. Much of what we know about events connected with Charles derives from this correspondence.

The Making of a Regiment

The transformation of the officers and recruits of the Voltigeurs into an efficient fighting force took a good deal of organization, training, and discipline.

The basic organization of the Corps can be outlined as follows:

```
                                    ┌ Major
                                    │                    ┌ Sergeant-
                                    │                    │ Major
                                    │
                                    │  Adjutant ─────────┤
  Captain        ┐                  │                    │
  Lieutenant     │                  │                    └ Bugle-Major
  Ensign         │                  │
                 │  Each            ┤
  Sergeant       ┤  Company         │  Paymaster ────────[ Pay Sergeant
                 │  (Originally six)│
  Corporal       │                  │  Surgeon ──────────[ Surgeon mate
  Privates       ┘                  │                    ┌ Sgt Armourer
                                    └  Quartermaster ────┤
                                                         └ Sgt Q.M.
```

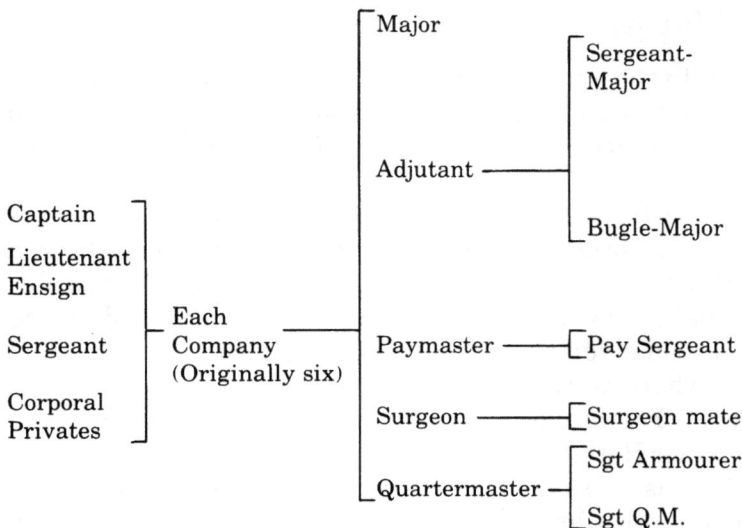

Many of the officers were friends or relatives of de
Salaberry, and this posed some initial problems because
a few of them tended to be lazy and disrespectful. It did
not take them too long to learn that, however pleasant
he might be socially, their new commander was a very
serious soldier. They soon responded to his leadership and
threw themselves into preparing the Corps for action.

The officers followed a busy schedule. They had to
continue recruiting, participate in training and drilling
their men, lead them on parade, do the bookkeeping for
the Company, go after deserters, sit on Courts Martial,
etc.; and when one was Duty Officer he had to inspect the
piquets, and guards, visit the hospital, check the men's
food, and keep everything running smoothly.

Deserters were not a big problem for the Voltigeurs,
but de Salaberry was a stern disciplinarian and deserters
were followed and brought back. Jacques Viger, who later
became one of de Salaberry's greatest admirers, wrote
home in May 1812 indicating that the commander was a
hard taskmaster and impossible to please.

The story is told[2] that on one occasion de Salaberry
entered the drill hall to find it in a state of pandemonium.
Rouleau, a troublemaker who was always looking for a
fight, was stripped to the waist and creating havoc. The
officers could do nothing to restore order. De Salaberry
roared at Rouleau to get dressed. Rouleau yelled back

that he would like to see the man who could make him do it. The words were hardly out of his mouth when de Salaberry's hand landed on his shoulder in a vice-like grip. He was flung to the floor so violently that the men fully expected him to go right through it. As soon as he was able to get up, he hurried to get properly dressed.

As the men came to see that his strict discpline applied to the officers as well as to themselves, and that while he was tough he was also just, they began to take a soldier's pride in their commander. Their camp songs started to reflect the esprit de corps that was developing. One of the songs began:

> C'est notre Major
> Qu'a le diable au corps,
> Qui nous donn'ra la mort.
> Y'a pas de loup ni tigre
> Qui soit si rustique.
> Sous la candeur du ciel
> Y'a pas son pareil.

Liberally translated this crude verse might run:

> There's our Colonel
> With Satan in his soul
> Who'll be the death of us all.
> There is no beast of prey
> That would dare stand in his way;
> And no matter how far you seek,
> You'll find our Colonel is unique.

The normal day for the men in training began when the bugler sounded reveille. There was a morning parade followed by target practice and squad manoeuvres. The afternoon was given over to normal fatigue duties and a late parade followed by supper.

The muzzle-loading Brown Bess was their principal arm, and they drilled until handling it became second nature:

1. Open the pan
2. Bite top off cartridge
3. Prime and close the pan
4. Load

5. Draw the ramrod, reverse it, put the broad end in the muzzle
6. Ram down the cartridge
7. Return the ramrod
8. Make ready
9. Present and fire.

Both the use and the care of weapons was critical for the soldiers and Regimental Orders were issued to ensure proper practices. In the Orders of 8 September 1812 it is specified that the Voltigeurs were forbidden to use their bayonets to tighten screws on their muskets or for any other purpose that could damage them.

The growing skill and confidence of the recruits testified to the value of the discipline and training. Not only did they individually become soldiers, but collectively they became a unit ready for combat.

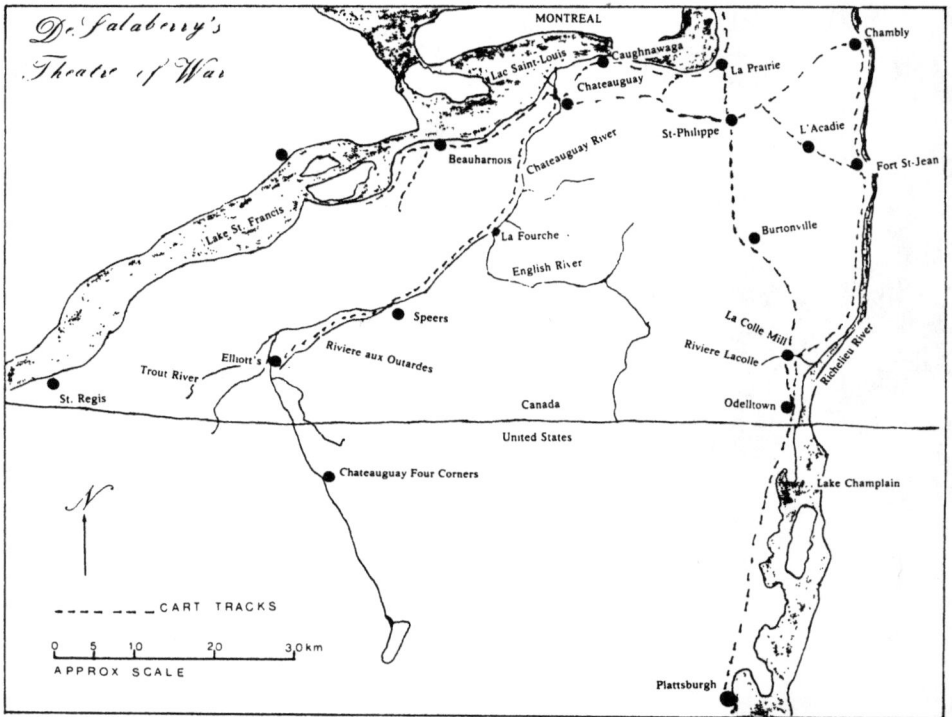

De Salaberry's Theatre of War.

Chapter Five

The War Begins

The Canadian Strategy

There were three general theatres of war during the War of 1812: Upper Canada, Lower Canada, and the high seas. On the seas both the Americans and British sent out privateers and their navies to raid enemy merchantmen. The British were hampered by their preoccupation with the war against Napoleon in Europe which severely restricted the strength of their naval squadron in North America until the last part of the war.

The Upper Canadian theatre was commanded by Major-General Sir Isaac Brock, an aggressive military leader who firmly believed that "the best defence is a good offence". He opened the war by capturing the American post at Michilimacinac. This aggressive attitude was due in large measure to the extensive frontier he had to defend and the very few troops with which he had to do it. Rather than stretch them piecemeal along that front, he protected his few strategic bases such as Kingston, St Joseph Island and Amherstburg and concentrated as many men as he could into a striking force. This force could both move quickly to a threatened area and threaten American posts at any time, thereby keeping the Americans off balance.

In Lower Canada the situation was considerably different. The St Lawrence River was the lifeline for supplies and reinforcements to Upper Canada and had to be kept open. Montreal, which controlled access to the upper St Lawrence, is perilously close to the American border. Given these factors, the commander, Lieutenant-General Sir George Prevost, adopted a more defensive strategy.

As soon as he was informed that President Madison had declared war (18 June 1812), he established a cordon of troops extending from Saint-Jean to Laprairie for the protection of Montreal. De Salaberry was sent to establish more advanced posts along the forty-fifth parallel from Saint-Regis to Yamaska. Operating from his headquarters in Saint-Philippe de Laprairie, he sent out strong piquets along the Lacolle and Chateauguay rivers, to cover the likely invasion routes. The most direct route for an American invasion was along the Richelieu River, but this was the best guarded and therefore the least likely route for the enemy to take. Throughout the war de Salaberry had charge of these advanced posts and commanded the first line of defence in this theatre.

In addition to four companies of his Voltigeurs, he had under his command part of the regular troops: all the Sedentary Militia bordering on the frontier, some battalions of Embodied Militia, and all the Indians. The number of Indians varied greatly from time to time and was usually between 80 and 250; the actual number of Iroquois and Algonquins under any given officer's command is difficult to ascertain but one authority gives Captain Joseph Maurice Lamothe 22 of them and Captain de Léry 150.[1]

The American Strategy

The American strategy for 1812 was devised by their Commander-in-Chief, Henry Dearborn, a veteran of the Revolutionary War. He planned three coordinated assaults.

The first would be in the West across the Detroit River. It was to be followed by one across the Niagara River and finally Dearborn himself would lead an offensive against Montreal. It is difficult to see what merit he found in this plan. If the various assaults were successful, the British would be retreating eastward, shortening their lines, improving their communications, and increasing their concentration of both men and materiel, while the Americans would be doing exactly the opposite. In the final assault, therefore, the Americans would be at their weakest and the British at their strongest.

On 11 July 1812 the first assault was led by another veteran of the Revolutionary War, General Hull, across the Detroit River. Once on the Canadian side he secured his beachhead and remained there. His communications by land were constantly threatened by Indians and those by water were disrupted and often intercepted by the Provincial Marine. Exactly a month after he invaded, he relinquished his beachhead and the last of his forces withdrew across the river to Detroit. Hot on his heels was General Brock with a small force. On 16 August Hull, terrified at the possibility of an Indian massacre, surrendered Detroit without a battle and was taken prisoner with his men. When he was paroled, Hull returned home to face a court-martial for his conduct of the campaign and was sentenced to be shot. A pardon saved him from that final humiliation.

The American assault on the Niagara frontier was led by General Stephen Van Rensselaer. In mid-October he crossed the Niagara River and fought his way to the top of Queenston Heights. Brock rushed to the site and rallied the small force there. Without waiting for the reinforcements that were en route he led a reckless charge up the escarpment. He was shot just above the heart and, despite his recklessness, is considered a major hero of the war.

His successor in command, General Sheaffe, organized the reinforcements as they came in and worked his way through the woods to the top of the hill. The New York militia had refused, as was their right, to leave that state and heavy casualties and dwindling supplies of ammunition forced the Americans to surrender. Among the 958 prisoners were a Brigadier and five Lieutenant-Colonels. His campaign a disaster, General Van Rensselaer resigned.

In the Lower Canadian theatre, the American Commander-in-Chief was Major-General Dearborn. In November he took command of troops assembled at several stations on Lake Champlain and began the campaign against Montreal.

Having received intelligence of this, de Salaberry prepared his defences. Bridges were destroyed and roads were obstructed with felled trees. Owing to the harsh weather, he had already put many of his troops into winter quarters, but had done so without removing them from their original positions of defence. By 17 November it was ascertained that Dearborn was advancing on Odelltown with about 6,000 men and a considerable train of field artillery. To meet this threat de Salaberry stationed about 400 men, comprising two companies of Voltigeurs, a detachment of local militia, and some Indians, behind the Lacolle River.

Dearborn sent ahead a strong advance guard of two infantry regiments and a troop of dragoons, numbering in all between 600 and 1,000 men under the command of Colonel Zebulon Pike.[2] They crossed the border on the night of 19 November with the intention of surprising the British outposts.

At four o'clock next morning the British Officer of the Day was making a routine inspection of piquets along the Lacolle River. He spotted the Americans fording the river in two divisions, one above and one below the outpost. The strength of the piquet was limited to 24 militiamen under Captain Panet and 15 Indians under Captain McCoy. Before they could retire, the post was almost surrounded and a volley fired into it at such short range that it caught fire. However, they returned the volley with one of their own and made good their escape under cover of the smoke and darkness.

Unknown to Pike, a group of New York militiamen had also crossed the river for the purpose of taking the outpost, and were ignorant of the fact that Pike was there. In the dark and confusion, the attackers fired at each other and maintained a heated battle among themselves until the morning light revealed their mistake. In the meantime, de Salaberry, having raised the "hue and cry", arrived at the scene with 102 men of the *avant guarde* of the Voltigeurs. They were determined to prevent the enemy from reaching their first main objective, L'Acadie.

Confused, disheartened and now faced with another fight, the Americans withdrew. Two days later the entire American army recrossed the frontier and retired into winter quarters. The campaign was over. For their part in the action, in which they suffered no losses, the Canadians were thanked in General Orders (the Commander-in-Chief's official means of communication with the army at large).

The First Winter

Things were reasonably quiet during the winter of 1812-1813. De Salaberry took advantage of this time to step up recruiting in order to bring his numbers up to the required strength. By March the Voltigeurs had mustered 438 non-commissioned officers and men, and many other recruits had not yet been properly enlisted. The Corps was enlarged to eight companies, all of which were completed with men to spare. Shortly thereafter four of these companies were sent to Upper Canada under the command of Major Herriot. The remainder continued their outpost duty on the Chateauguay and Lacolle rivers.

The only real soldiering that the Corps did was in February when Prevost ordered de Salaberry to take four companies of Voltigeurs to join the force preparing an attack on the Salmon River. When they reached Coteau-du-Lac, Colonel Scott called off the expedition and there was nothing for them to do but turn around and march back to winter quarters. Actually, a number of Voltigeurs had already participated in an attack on Salmon River on 23 November 1812, when they had captured a small fort from the Americans; that was their baptism of fire.

The lessons of 1812 were not lost on the Americans. The Secretary of War, Dr Eustis (a dentist) resigned and was replaced by the much more aggressive General John Armstrong. He retained Dearborn but took over the strategic planning himself.

1813 in Upper Canada

The American plans for 1813 against Upper Canada called for General Harrison to pin down the British, under General Proctor, in the West while Dearborn was to successively capture Kingston, York (Toronto) and Fort George in the Niagara area.

The campaign in the West was a British disaster. Their fleet on Lake Erie was soundly beaten and Proctor's army virtually destroyed. At the battle of Moraviantown, Tecumseh, their Indian ally was killed and Proctor barely escaped with his life. Harrison did not follow up this success but withdrew with his men to Detroit, having achieved the first major success by American arms during the war.

The plans for Dearborn's campaign were changed because the American naval commander on Lake Ontario, Commodore Chauncey, was well aware of the strength of the defences at Kingston. Instead they sailed directly to York, captured it, and burned the provincial parliament buildings. They then moved to the Niagara frontier.

The British here were heavily outnumbered but they put up a terrific fight and suffered heavy casualties before General Vincent spiked the guns, blew up the magazine and led an orderly withdrawal as far as Burlington Heights. Here he turned around and with the help of British naval gunnery drove the pursuing Americans back to Fort George where he kept them penned in while the British conducted a number of successful raids on the American side of the river.

Eventually the Americans fired the town of Newark and abandoned Fort George. The British pursued them to the American side, surprised and captured their Fort Niagara and continued on the offensive. In retaliation for the burning of York and Newark, they captured and destroyed every American post on the Niagara frontier, including the town of Buffalo. By the end of the year the whole American side of the frontier was a blackened ruin.

Chapter Six

The Campaign
Against Montreal
1813

Preparations on de Salaberry's Front

Without the pressure of an immediate threat to his frontier, de Salaberry spent much of the spring and summer of 1813 at his headquarters in Saint Philippe. He trained his troops, sent out his patrols, probed the enemy strength and activities, evaluated the intelligence reports, and supervised the endless staff work that is necessary to an army in the field.

His wife, Marie-Anne, was with him in Saint Philippe and in May of that year their first child, Melchior Alphonse, was born.

During that summer the British flotilla on Lake Champlain was sent out to harass the enemy. They burned the barracks at Swanton, Vermont, and Plattsburg and destroyed two blockhouses at Champlain, New York. De Salaberry and the Voltigeurs covered their return to base down the Richelieu river.

American Plans

The threat to Lower Canada in 1813 began on 23 July when Armstrong submitted his plans to President Madison. Kingston was to have been the main target, but again its strong defences discouraged the attempt. Instead, it was determined to capture Montreal. General John Armstrong the American Secretary of War, himself assessed the situation well:

At Montreal, however, we find the weaker place, the smallest force to encounter . . . you hold a position which completely severs the enemy's line of operations and which, while it restrains all below, withers and perishes all above itself.[1]

To carry out this campaign against Montreal he planned to use two armies.

Major-General James Wilkinson was selected as senior commander for the campaign. He arrived at Sackett's Harbour on Lake Ontario in August and set about raising and preparing an army of about 7,000 men. They were to move directly on Montreal via the St Lawrence Valley.

The second army was brought together at Burlington, Vermont under Major-General Wade Hampton with Brigadier George Izard as second-in-command. They were to cut through from the Champlain Valley and join forces with the first army just south of Montreal. Together they would constitute by far the largest force that the Americans had directed against any objective in this war. The British had no force of comparable size with which to stop them. If they reached Montreal, the city would have to surrender.

It was a strange leadership team that Armstrong had put together for this campaign. Major-General James Wilkinson was an inveterate political intriguer. During the Revolutionary War he was involved with the "Conway Cabal" that tried to remove Washington from command of the army and replace him with Gates. While active in American politics, he took a pension from Spain for trying to promote the secession of part of the western United States, making it a satellite of the Spanish empire. He was also involved with the infamous Aaron Burr in an attempt to set up a separate republic; but he decided to betray Burr. He has been stigmatized as being "a traitor to every cause he embraced".[2]

The army forming on de Salaberry's front was led by Major-General Hampton. Most of his military experience had been as a guerrilla under Sumter and "The Swamp Fox", Francis Marian during the Revolutionary War. Now, at 59, he was one of the richest men in the South with several thousand slaves on his immense plantations. *The Dictionary of American Biography* characterizes him as a man whose

> many political and military responsibilities had not
> kept him from advancing his private interests. . . .
> (he had) the frontiersman's attitude toward land;
> that is the will to possess it without an overscru-
> pulous regard for the means of acquiring possession.

Fortunately for the American cause, Hampton's second-in-command was a considerably more capable and reliable officer. Brigadier-General George Izard was the son of a prominent South Carolinian family and had received the good, liberal education typical of gentlemen of that era, including the European tour. After about ten years as an American artillery officer, he left to undertake further military studies in both England and France. At the outbreak of this war he was promoted to Colonel in the 2nd U.S. Artillery, and the following year to Brigadier with responsibility for the defenses of New York. For the current campaign he was in charge of training Hampton's troops, many of whom had been part of Dearborn's force in the 1812 campaign. His performance at Chateauguay earned him a promotion to Major-General.

Hampton also had a good senior infantry officer in Colonel Robert Purdy, a Pennsylvanian. His early soldiering was done against the Indians on the Ohio frontier under the rigorous training and strict discipline of Major-General Anthony Wayne.

Disposition of the Canadian Forces

The threat posed by Hampton's gathering army had a startling effect on Prevost. There was almost constant movement of troops throughout the whole area.

In Montreal, the defenders were reinforced by a detachment of the 19th Light Dragoons and two 24-pound cannons from Laprairie, as well as a detachment of Royal Marines from Trois Rivières. All militia from the north shore of the St Lawrence within 80 kilometres of Montreal were ordered there with arms and earthworking tools.

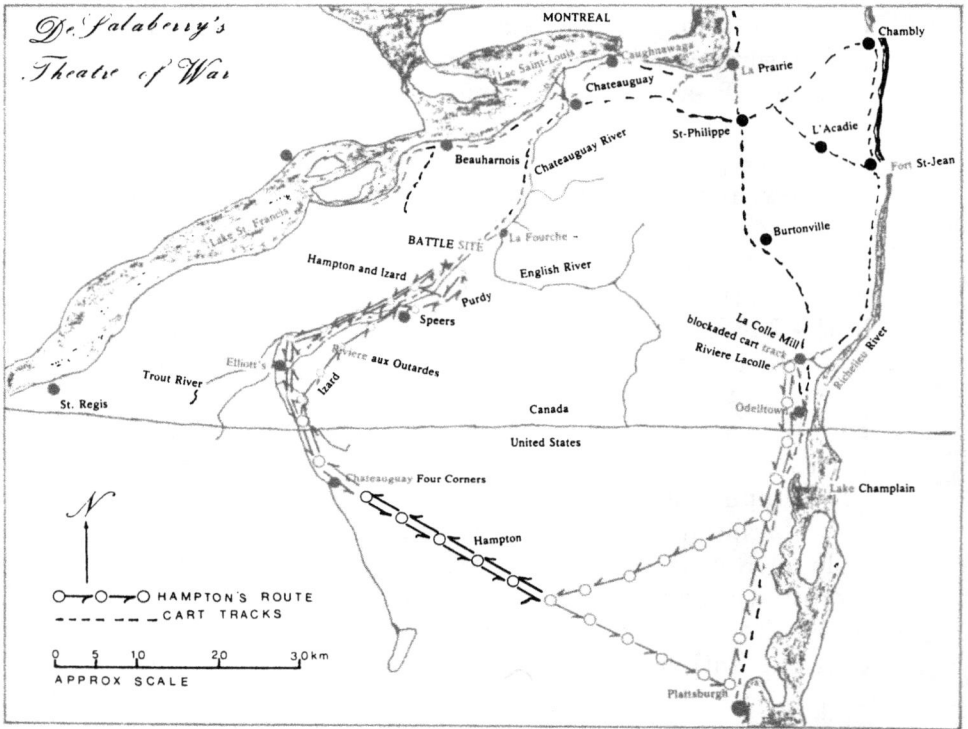

De Salaberry's Theatre of War

MONTREAL
Chambly
Lac Saint-Louis
Caughnawaga
La Prairie
Chateauguay
L'Acadie
Beauharnois
Chateauguay River
St-Philippe
Fort St-Jean
Lake St. Francis
BATTLE SITE
La Fourche
Burtonville
Hampton and Izard
English River
Purdy
Speers
La Colle Mill
blockaded cart track
Elliott's
Riviere aux Outardes
Riviere Lacolle
Richelieu River
Trout River
Izard
St. Regis
Canada
Odelltown
United States
Chateauguay Four Corners
Lake Champlain
N
Hampton
○—?—○—→○ HAMPTON'S ROUTE
– – – – – – CART TRACKS
0   5   10   20   30 km
APPROX SCALE
Plattsburgh

General Hampton's movements in October 1813.

All troops were to carry two days worth of provisions in their packs at all times.

Coteau-du-Lac, at the Beauharnois Channel, a post well-placed to impede an army coming down the St Lawrence, was manned by several companies of the 103rd Foot, backed up by some Indians and local militia (2nd Battalion [Beauharnois] Sedentary Militia). Any militia units from the area that were not already under orders were brought in to take reserve positions.

With all this movement of troops, the British were still extremely weak and, in fact, other than calling in a few militia units, all that had been done was to weaken some parts of the defensive line to strengthen others.

De Salaberry had no intention of allowing American intelligence to get any clear idea of how small his force actually was; so he kept up a fairly constant movement of troops all along his front. For example, one of the units involved in this screen was the Canadian Fencibles, whose marches took them from Chambly to Plattsburg, New York, back to Chambly, to Laprairie, then to Saint Philippe, from there to Douglas Settlement near the lines, back to Saint Philippe and then to Saint Pierre. This kind of patrolling in strength did more than screen their actual numbers. It also helped the morale of people living in the areas because they had a chance to see their defenders.

Hampton Invades Canada

Hampton's first move of the campaign was to transfer his entire force across Lake Champlain to Plattsburgh. This operation took ten days and was completed by 18 September. It surprised Prevost who had been expecting a northward thrust; he became convinced that Hampton would continue westward to join Wilkinson for an attack on Kingston. Leaving Sir Roger Sheaffe in command at Montreal, he hurried upriver to Kingston to consolidate the defenses there.

Meanwhile, on the nineteenth, Hampton ordered his forces northward. They were preceded by the Light Corps and flanked on the right by the Navy. The British immediately blocked up the roads around Odelltown and tore down the bridge across the Lacolle River. At midnight, Hampton ordered the main body of his troops to halt at Chazy, New York. Without any effort at making camp, his men slept on their arms. Hampton wanted them to be up soon after sunrise, and on the march again to Champlain, at the foot of the lake, and on down the Richelieu River for another four miles.

The advance troops which had travelled by boat landed above Odelltown and marched on that village in two columns under Snelling and Hamilton. At one o'clock in the morning Snelling surprised a British piquet and, after a brief fight, he drove it in, killing three men and capturing six. Soon, Hamilton arrived, and by nine o'clock the entire American army was in and around Odelltown.

De Salaberry had too few men to mount a counterattack against a force the size of Hampton's, but he determined to contain them until he could obtain reinforcements. He sent out Indian patrols under Captain Gamelin-Gaucher and they, in fact, struck the first blows when they ambushed and dispersed an American patrol. Fear of Indians kept subsequent American patrols from probing too far from camp and discovering how few men de Salaberry actually had.

He sent Major Joseph-François Perrault with a company of the 4th Battalion Embodied Militia to begin the defensive operations and joined him soon afterwards with 150 Voltigeurs. They increased the abbatis, blocked the roads with fallen trees, threw up wooden entrenchments, and continually harassed the Americans.

Surprised by de Salaberry's defensive moves, Hampton realized that he might be in for a much more difficult campaign than he had envisioned. After a day and a half he called a council of war with his officers to consider the situation. They were unable to probe effectively de Salaberry's strength; they might have to fight every foot of the way because the roads were blocked and to top it all off, they had insufficient supplies, especially of water. The council recommended a withdrawal back into the United States so that they could improve their supply system and, having done that, attempt to reach Montreal through the Chateauguay Valley.

In late September many of the streams were virtually dry and even the Lacolle River was low. While the Americans were worried about lack of water as a supply, de Salaberry was concerned because this gave considerable tactical advantage to the invader: it made it easier for the Americans to move wherever they chose, and it reduced the effectiveness of the rivers and streams as natural defenses.

The Americans slowly fell back to Chazy. On 23 September they began marching westward to Four Corners at the head of the Chateauguay Valley. The logistics of Hampton's force were so ineffectual that it was able to bring with it only the barest essentials. Some of his officers, especially Purdy, were extremely critical of his mishandling of the whole supply situation.

They covered the 110 kilometres to Four Corners in about three days. After establishing a camp, Hampton started building and improving a roadway back to his supply base at Plattsburg. He was quite far from his stores there and without water transportation this would be the only way he could bring forward the artillery and the supplies he needed.

Reconnaissance and Harassment.

De Salaberry's scouts were quick to report Hampton's movements as he withdrew from Odelltown. As soon as it was clear that the whole American army was moving westward, de Salaberry led the bulk of his troops in a forced march of 24 hours to cover the next most likely invasion route, the Chateauguay Valley. He left patrols along the way to protect against any possible incursions by enemy patrols and to keep open the line of communications along his whole front. He set up his own headquarters in a newly built stone tavern on the banks of the Chateauguay, three kilometres below Sainte Martine.

As the Americans settled in at Four Corners they found little comfort. Their supplies were low, their worn-out light summer uniforms were inadequate for the damp and cold of autumn, and the night had its own terrors for those on sentry duty. Hidden by the dark were small units of de Salaberry's forces, many of them Indians, and every night shots would ring out somewhere around the periphery of the camp. So effective was this sniping and harassment that the sentries built small blockhouses for themselves and did not dare to venture out in the dark. Their food had to be hauled from Plattsburg, and kept about 1,000 oxen busy pulling 400 wagons back and forth continually. Poor weather inevitably delayed delivery so that morale, never particularly high, continued to deteriorate. Finally, their sagging sense of security was shattered in the late afternoon of 1 October when de Salaberry penetrated their defenses in a surprise raid.

Prevost ordered him to lead a quixotic attack with about 200 soldiers and some Indians. Considering the numerical superiority of the American army and the fact that they were in a fortified camp, it seems likely that Prevost, whose hostility to de Salaberry dated from the recruiting years in England, was trying to discredit his military reputation. De Salaberry, himself, suggested in his personal correspondence that Prevost seemed to be trying to get rid of him. Whatever the reason for the order, de Salaberry was quick to obey.

As they cautiously approached the American camp, the Canadians lost the element of surprise when an Indian prematurely fired on a sentry. De Salaberry reacted quickly by leading one company of Voltigeurs and the Indians in a rush through the outer defences. The Americans rallied and tried to outflank the attackers. Twice the Indians withdrew and twice de Salaberry brought them back; but this was not the style of fighting for which they were trained and finally they bolted, taking most of the Voltigeurs with them.

This left de Salaberry with Captain Chevalier Duchesnay and three Voltigeurs to look after themselves as the Americans counterattacked. For half an hour they skirmished, until dusk arrived and they were able to slip back through the American lines. That night they camped in the woods with the rest of their men whom they met seven kilometres to the rear.

The next morning de Salaberry tried to organize a further reconaissance of the camp, but the Indians would not participate. Without them his force was too weak to justify the attempt. Frustrated, he ordered a slow return down the cart track along the Chateauguay River, and blocked the road with felled trees as he went. Thus, if Hampton chose this route for an advance, he would have difficulty clearing the road for his artillery and horses.

De Salaberry was well aware that Hampton could move either northward via the Chateauguay or westward to the St Lawrence, but that the Chateauguay afforded by far the shorter and more direct route. Hampton tried a ruse to draw off the defenders. He sent a force eastward to attack a small settlement on Mississquoi Bay; but this was so pointless that no one was fooled.

Every day that Hampton delayed meant an extra day for de Salaberry to shape up his meagre defences, encourage his men, and establish plans for the best use of the terrain. He blocked the road, destroyed bridges, and set up piquets in small block houses and abbatis. He set up advance posts at the junction of each of two tributaries with the Chateauguay and put them under the command of Major Henry of the Beauharnois Sedentary Militia. Henry's base was at La Fourche (near the present town of Howick) where the English River flows into the Chateauguay; his other post was at Spear's (near Ormstown) where the Outarde River joins it. Between these two posts lay an area composed of a series of ravines that de Salaberry had chosen for his battlefield.

Hampton's Second Invasion

On 16 October Hampton received orders from Armstrong to advance to the mouth of the Chateauguay. About 1,500 of his militia refused to leave their state and were detailed to guard the supply route to Plattsburg and the stores at Four Corners. Five days after receiving the orders, the lead units of the American army finally crossed the Canadian border.

The blocked roads were an effective deterrent, and Hampton sent a large work party ahead of the main body of his army to cut a practical road through the twenty kilometres of woods to their first objective, Spear's. Brigadier Izard led one line regiment and some light troops in a flanking movement to capture the piquet there and to secure the area as an advanced base for the army.

Izard's move was a complete success. At about 4 p.m. on 21 October his troops attacked and captured the piquet on the north shore of the Chateauguay. The small squad of militia and about ten Indians were surprised as they were preparing dinner outside their blockhouse. Those who managed to slip away hurried downriver to Major Henry with the news.

Henry sent the report on to de Salaberry and immediately ordered the two flank companies of the 5th Battalion Select Embodied Militia (under Captains Levesque and de Bartzch) with about 200 of his Beauharnois Sedentary Militia to move upriver and occupy the site de Salaberry had chosen for his major defensive position. By nightfall these men were camped near the edge of the hardwood bush about five kilometres below the ravines. Next morning de Salaberry arrived with two companies of Voltigeurs and Ferguson's Light Company of the Canadian Fencibles. With the militia units, they moved on, occupied the ravine, and began setting up their defensive works. Soon after they arrived, an American patrol was sighted and the awareness of how close the enemy was helped speed up the preparation of the defenses.

After two days of work on the principal breastworks, de Salaberry sent out work parties of the Sedentary Militia under Captain Longuetin to build an abbatis or log entanglement in advance of his position, and to clear the field of fire in front of these positions. Longuetin had his men kneel as he led them in a short prayer and then, rising, he told them that having fulfilled their duty to God, they would now fulfill their duty to the king. They were covered by a piquet of Voltigeurs and a few Fencibles as they worked.

Meanwhile, Hampton's main body of troops reached the advance position at Spear's on the twenty-second and spent the next two days improving the road and bringing forward their artillery and stores. At the same time they improved the ford in the river thereby building it up with coarse gravel. The blocked roads had given de Salaberry the time he needed to prepare his position.

SWAMPY WOODS

AMERICAN CAMP

INDIANS AND BUGLERS

SWAMPY WOODS

Artillery

AMERICAN COLUMN

Capt. Lamothe

INDIANS

Capt. Ferguson

Gen. Hampton

Capt. C.J. Duchesnay

Capt. de Lery

Col. de Salaberry

VOLTIGEURS

Chateauguay River

Farm Fields

Lt-Col. McDonell

Capt. L. Juchereau

Capt. Lecuyer

SEDENTARY MILITIA

SWAMPY WOODS

AMERICAN COLUMN

Col. McCarthy

Capt. Rouville

Capt. Lonctin

FENCIBLES

Lt-Col. Malhiot

VOLTIGEURS

Capt. Laveque

PIQUET

INCORPORATED MILITIA

ABATTIS

Capt. de Tonnancour

Observation Company

Ford

PIQUET

INCORPORATED MILITIA

INCORPORATED MILITIA

Capt. Bruyere

Capt. Daly

SWAMPY WOODS

ABATTIS

CANADIAN CAMP

The Battle Plan of Chateauguay as de Salaberry reported it shortly after the battle.

82

Chapter Seven

The Battle of Chateauguay

De Salaberry Prepares for Battle

The site de Salaberry had chosen as his battlefield was the best possible one along the entire length of the Chateauguay River. Half a dozen gullies or ravines crossed the area. He fortified each of them with log breastworks running from the bank of the river, across the cleared fields on either side of the road and into the woods and swamp on the right flank. About two kilometres in advance of the first line were two small abbatis in a position to slow down the American advance and to alert the main forces that the enemy was on its way. The woods on the right flank in advance of de Salaberry's lines provided cover for some of the Indians and a few buglers.

Behind the main line of defence on Bryson's Ravine was Grant's Ford; this could provide the Americans with access to the left flank. But the weakness was covered with breastworks on both banks of the river, and another abbatis was erected a little upriver on the swampy and wooded south side to help break up any attack on the ford itself.

Closer to the American camp, de Salaberry had small groups of men from various units marching as though to reinforce him. As soon as they were out of sight of the Americans, they reversed their tunics, hurried back to where they had started and reappeared, giving the illusion of many different units concentrating on the Chateauguay. The ruse worked: Hampton reported to Armstrong that "the enemy is hourly adding to his strength".[1]

One group of reinforcements actually did arrive. The 1st Light Battalion of Select Embodied Militia under Lt Colonel (Red) George Macdonell was ordered from Kingston

to Chateauguay on 21 October. They brought together all
the flat-bottomed scows and bateaux they could find and
set off down the St Lawrence. It was a rough trip what
with wind, rain and the rapids at Long Sault, the Cedars
and Cascades. They ran into a bad storm as they entered
Lake St Louis, but were able to land at Beauharnois late
on 24 October. As soon as they were ashore, they set off
on a trail leading to the Chateauguay and arrived at de
Salaberry's position during the morning of the next day.
De Salaberry was delighted to see them and placed them
in a reserve position at Morrison's Ford, four or five kilometres downstream. Macdonell himself was placed in
charge of the reserve positions.

When everything was ready, Major-General de
Watteville, de Salaberry's superior officer, came forward
and inspected the field. He was impressed with the prep-
arations and dispositions, and he had no suggestions to
make for any improvements.

The American Tactics

The Americans now had a good idea of where de Salaberry
was, and since they were using some American-born settlers of that area as guides, they also knew of Grant's
Ford behind the defenses on Bryson's Ravine. Major-
General Hampton decided on a two-pronged attack. One
column was to push through the swamps and bush of the
south side of the river to the ford and take de Salaberry
in the flank, while the main body launched a frontal assault. The sound of firing from the flanking column was
to be the signal for the main attack.

At sunset on 25 October Colonel Purdy led the flanking column out of the American camp, across to the south
shore of the Chateauguay and into the dark woods. His
force was made up of three regular infantry regiments,
the 4th, 33rd, and 34th as well as some volunteer and light
companies. His guides protested that they did not know
their way through the swamps, but Hampton was ada-
mant that they lead the way.

Throughout the night the column struggled, often in
single file, through the wet, entangled maze. As the sun

Col. (Red) George Macdonell

came up the next morning they found that they had only advanced about ten kilometres. Wet, tired, and frustrated they pushed on downriver.

While Purdy was trying to reach the ford with about half the army, Hampton ordered Izard to mobilize the main force. Early in the morning of Tuesday, 26 October, Izard sent ahead his advance guard, and then the infantry and dragoons. As they neared the Canadian positions, they listened intently for the sound of firing that would indicate Purdy's contact at the ford.

The Battle Is Joined

That morning the advance abbatis was commanded by Lieutenant Johnson of the Voltigeurs. A party of Beauharnais' axmen working in advance of it was covered by Lieutenant Guy with 20 of his Voltigeurs and ten Fencibles. When the American advance guard came into view along the cart track, Guy had his men lay down a covering fire as the axemen withdrew behind the abbatis; he then ordered his own men to fall back to the same position.

As soon as de Salaberry heard the firing he ordered up four companies and led them to the abbatis. Guy and Johnson had maintained fire on the Americans, who were now visible in large numbers. Quickly, de Salaberry deployed his men along the line. Captain Lamothe and about 20 Indians went to the extreme right of the abbatis and extended beyond it in an arc curving forward to face the American flank. To their left was Captain Ferguson's Light Fencible Company with 72 men, some of whom were sent forward as skirmishers. Next to them and holding the centre of the line was Captain J.B. Juchereau Duchesnay's Voltigeur Company; it was flanked by Captain M.L. Juchereau Duchesnay whose Voltigeurs covered the junction of the abbatis and the river, and were positioned in an arc curving to the rear of the line. Each Voltigeur Company had about 70 men. Finally came a company of 66 Beauharnais militiamen under Captain Longuetin; they faced directly onto the river.

The Americans made no move to take the position because Hampton was waiting for Purdy's signal. Still,

86

they looked like a considerable threat as they waited in full view but out of range of the vastly outnumbered Canadians. De Salaberry moved quietly among his men, calling them by their names, encouraging them, and allaying their fears. His capacity for remembering names stood him in good stead and helped to reduce the impersonal nature of military leadership which was always frightening to militiamen. Thinking no one was watching, one of the men tried to sneak off into the woods only to find de Salaberry blocking the path. All that de Salaberry said was "Is that what you came here for, Jerome?"

Meanwhile de Salaberry had alerted Macdonell to the threat posed by Purdy on the other bank of the river. The defenses there consisted of Captain Bruyère's company of Chateauguay Chasseurs, numbering about 40 men, who were covering the ford. Macdonell had immediately ordered two companies to Bruyère's support. They crossed the ford at about 11 o'clock. Some distance in advance of the position, Bruyère had met Purdy's advance guard of two infantry companies, and after a brief exchange of fire had started to retire to the prepared position near the ford. The arrival of the reinforcements, however, changed the situation: while de Tonnancour with his 70 men held the abbatis there as a reserve, Daly and Bruyère, now 90 strong, went forward to meet the Americans and forced the advance guard to retreat.

While both Hampton and de Salaberry awaited anxiously word from the south bank, Purdy's main force was just a little upriver of the main abbatis and his retreating men were approaching the river bank. Not only were they surprised at the sharp resistance they had met but, looking across the river they caught glimpses of the reserve lines, giving an exaggerated impression of de Salaberry's strength. Purdy reported this news to Hampton along with word of his own impasse.

There was only sporadic firing on both sides of the river as both American columns waited for something to happen. Finally, around two o'clock, the noise of musketry broke out again on the south shore as Daly and Bruyère engaged Purdy's men in a series of sharp squad actions.

Hampton decided that it was now or never and ordered Izard to advance on the abbatis. As the enormous

American column came within range, a large officer gal-
lopped forward and called out to the Canadians in French:
"Brave Canadians, surrender, we have no wish to ʌurt
you." De Salaberry grabbed a musket from one of his men,
leaped up on a stump, and shot the man. This began the
action. Canadian buglers sounded the "commence firing"
and the abbatis roared with musketry.

Izard swung his column to the left in line, facing the
abbatis and had his men pour volley after volley into the
defenses. Noting the strength of the centre and left of the
abbatis, he concentrated on the right and drove in the
Fencible skirmishers. As the skirmishers withdrew behind the abbatis, the Americans, thinking they had turned
the flank, gave a great shout and charged forward.

De Salaberry was quick to realize the critical moment and, still mounted on his stump, he ordered his men
to return the shout. It was picked up along the line and
then by the Indians in the woods on the American left
flank. Before the cheering was done, he had his buglers
in the woods sound the advance. Macdonell in the reserve
line had all his buglers take up the call.

The Americans had thought they were on the verge
of victory. Now they felt as though the entire British
army was before them and all the Indians east of the
Rockies hidden in the woods to their left. The initiative
that could have carried them over the abbatis was gone.

In the pause that followed, de Salaberry called across
the river to Daly warning him to speak French so that
the Americans could not understand. Daly tersely reported his situation: so far he and Bruyère had been fighting units on the fringes of Purdy's command but now the
Americans had organized sufficiently to form some kind
of firing line in the bush. De Salaberry shouted back that
he should try to get Purdy to the river bank where he
could provide supporting fire.

With outstanding courage, Daly led the two companies in a rush close to the American line. There they
stopped, dropped to one knee and delivered a volley. The
counter volley by the Americans was too high but it did
hit Captain Daly who was standing to direct his men's
fire. Despite the wound, Daly ordered a bayonet charge
and led his men to the line where he fell with a second

wound. Almost simultaneously Captain Bruyère was wounded. The command of the two companies now fell to Daly's Lieutenant, Benjamin Schiller.

But the Americans counterattacked, and Schiller ordered his men to retire. He himself picked up the wounded Daly and carried him to prevent his capture. An American officer rushed Schiller to try and capture both him and Daly, but Schiller was an aggressive soldier too. Placing Daly on the ground, he drew his sabre and ran forward to meet the American in a duel which ended abruptly when he decapitated his opponent. Stopping only to pick up Daly, he slowly led the withdrawal to the river bank.

The dense woods prevented the Americans from inflicting serious casualties; but they knew that Schiller would soon be stopped by the river, so they gathered for a final charge. Breaking clear of the trees at the bank, they were shocked to find themselves looking straight into the Canadian position across the river where de Salaberry, in plain view atop his stump, was calmly watching them through his telescope.

Speed was now critical to Purdy. He had to capture Schiller before de Salaberry could divert troops from his front line to cover this flank. Massing his men, he closed in on Schiller.

Schiller waited until the last possible minute before giving the order that his men should fall flat on their faces. At the same instant, Longuetin's and Duchesnay's companies, who had been completely concealed in the reeds and bushes across the river, opened a murderous fire into Purdy's ranks. As the Americans tried to return fire, Schiller moved his men downriver and attacked their flank. Caught in the crossfire, the American infantry broke and rushed for cover in the woods, leaving their casualties where they fell. Some of them tried to escape by swimming across the river to their other lines, but a few militiamen went in after them and hauled them ashore as prisoners.[2] It was now about 2:30 p.m. and half the American army, under Purdy, was effectively out of action for at least a few hours, and Lieutenant Schiller had won his Captaincy on the field.

De Salaberry expected Purdy to fall back up the river, cross over, and join Izard's column for a more determined assault on the abbatis. He was not surprised, then, when Izard, on Hampton's orders, slowly pulled his own men back, formed them into marching columns, and withdrew a few kilometres. They would likely return stronger than before. De Salaberry sent forward some Indian piquets, then took advantage of the lull to repair the damages of battle, pull back the men in relays for rest and food and generally keep their spirits up.

Schiller was ordered back to the ford where he was able to send on his wounded to the field hospital set up by two army surgeons further downstream in the Morrison farm house. In view of the action they had just been through, their losses were incredibly light. Captains Daly and Bruyère were wounded, and Daly had sustained only two killed, six wounded, and four missing.

The American Retreat

Purdy retired as far as a bend in the river called Round Point and set up a defensive position. He detailed a few work crews to build rafts. When they were completed he had his wounded ferried across to the far shore with a request for Hampton to provide a guard for them and to cover his own withdrawal across the river. He had a rude shock when he learned that the other column had already retired several kilometres further upstream and that his wounded were not, in fact, behind their own lines but in the no man's land between the two forces.

Realizing the danger from Indian patrols, Purdy quickly built a floating bridge from logs and debris along the bank and sent 100 men under Major Snelling to their support. As they crossed the makeshift bridge, Snelling's men came under fire from an Indian patrol but managed to get across, pick up their wounded, and hurry on to join up with the rear of Izard's column.

Many of the American wounded had been left on the battlefield before the abbatis and de Salaberry had had them brought in and sent back with his own wounded to the field hospital at Morrison's. His own casualties had been extremely light. The Fencibles had four wounded

Maj. Gen. Louis de Watteville

and three captured and the Voltigeur companies had four wounded.

After the Americans had withdrawn, Sir George Prevost and Major General de Watteville visited the front lines. Prevost gave what is officially described as an inspiring address. He was very reserved in his compliments to de Salaberry, gave de Watteville major credit for his "judicious arrangements", and praised the men for their courage. Because another attack was likely, the senior officers withdrew, de Watteville to Ste-Martine and Prevost to La Fourche. As dusk came on, the men remained in their front lines and took turns sleeping in their firing positions.

Purdy's men spent the night lying on the ground, surrounded by the dark swamp and woods. They were utterly exhausted, because they had had no sleep the previous night and then had been surprised by the stiff resistance of the Canadians. From time to time, shots would ring out in the woods as stragglers and patrolling Indians fired at sounds and shadows. Several times during the night patrols broke into their camp and took prisoners. To add to the general discomfort of both sides a heavy rain fell that night.

In the morning de Salaberry called up three companies from the reserves to reinforce the abbatis. He fully expected Hampton to attack again very soon.

There was much less activity in the American camp. Purdy managed to ford the river and rejoin Hampton, who then convened his officers in a council of war. They tried to assess their losses: Hampton reported a maximum of 50 killed, wounded, and missing. This was a very conservative estimate. Actually de Salaberry's men themselves buried about 40 Americans and held 36 prisoners; and the Americans had also buried some of their own dead. In any case, considering that Hampton had about 5,000 men at his immediate disposal, these losses would not noticeably affect his fighting strength. However, Hampton's council of war gave the unanimous opinion that they must withdraw to Four Corners. At noon the following day, 28 October, they began the march back to American soil.

A reconnaissance party under Colonel Hughes, a Royal Engineer, sent word of the withdrawal back to de Salaberry. De Salaberry quickly reinforced the patrols with a large party of Indians under Captain Lamothe and ordered Captain Rouville's company to participate in the pursuit of the enemy. Captain Debartzch was then sent with a company of Beauharnais militiamen to destroy the temporary bridges that the Americans had built. When they returned they were loaded down with discarded American equipment: 150 muskets and six drums were picked up along Purdy's line of march, as well as knapsacks, provisions, personal supplies, and the great variety of impedimenta that is discarded by an army in retreat. It was really the type of materiel brought back by Debartzch's men that gave de Salaberry his first clear indication of the mood of Hampton's men; it was surprisingly defeatist.

The next evening, 29 October, Hampton's army made camp at Piper's Road. As dusk fell, Captain Lamothe moved his Indians close to the camp and launched an attack on the perimeter that killed one of the sentries and wounded seven others. He then fell back into the dark woods where the Americans dared not follow. It was an uneasy night for the American soldiers, and as soon as possible in the morning they pulled out. Under the watchful eyes of an Indian party led by Captain Dominique Ducharme, they finally crossed the border back into their own country.

Wilkinson's Advance

One-half of the American campaign against Montreal had been stopped. The other army, under Major-General Wilkinson, was moving down the St Lawrence. On 11 November they had to turn to fight a rearguard action against Colonel Morrison and his 800 men, including three companies of Voltigeurs at John Crysler's farm. Morrison drove the Americans from the battlefield but did not succeed in blocking their route to Montreal. The following day Wilkinson received Hampton's report of the defeat at Chateauguay. On the strength of that, his officers agreed with him in a council of war to call off the campaign and retire into winter quarters on the American side of the river. The threat to Montreal was over.

looking for volunteers

Chapter Eight

The War Carries On

Prevost vs de Salaberry

With the battle clearly over, de Salaberry wrote his report to de Watteville. In it he commended those officers and men who had made outstanding contributions to the victory. He also sent a letter to his wife in Laprairie indicating that Prevost's attitude after the battle had been very "cool".

Knowing that his father-in-law, de Rouville, was also intensely interested, he sent him a letter detailing the battle. De Rouville quickly relayed the information to Louis de Salaberry and reminded him that it had been 38 years since the two of them had been taken prisoner after the long siege of Fort St-Jean. Three days later he wrote again to Louis saying that he had seen a sketch of the battle plan and that Prevost was attempting to discredit Charles.

On learning of the victory Louis' first reaction was pride in his son's achievement; but he was also concerned about the way Charles exposed himself to enemy fire. In his letter to Charles after the battle, he commented on the stump that his son had jokingly called his wooden horse:

> I acknowledge that there couldn't be a firmer and steadier mount under fire but not withstanding that I would advise and earnestly beg you to choose another horse. Perched on that you are only making a target of yourself. To face danger is worthy of a man of your character; but one need not look for opportunities to do it. You are, I believe, the first general to win battle while mounted on a stump. Believe me, change your mount![1]

97

bringing in the recruits

In the General Orders which Prevost issued on the day after the battle, he described de Salaberry's men as advance piquets of the British, thrown out for the purpose of protecting work parties. In his report to Lord Bathurst on 30 October Prevost went so far as to recommend the awarding of colours for the regiments involved at Chateauguay, although ordinarily light regiments were not entitled to colours. He made no particular reference, however, to either the Voltigeurs or de Salaberry and, in fact, claimed that he, himself, arrived at the front just after the action had commenced.

De Salaberry was taken aback by the extent of Prevost's misrepresentations. He had never before sought credit for his accomplishments but now he was determined that Prevost, who had hampered him at every turn, would not get credit for a victory towards which he had contributed nothing. To this end he sent a dispatch to the Adjutant-General succinctly outlining the facts:

Advance Posts November
1813

Sir,

Referring to the General Orders of the 27th issued in consequence of the action in which I repulsed General Hampton's army, I observe with regret that the choice of several positions which I defended is not attributed to me, neither is the disposition of the force which was immediately under my command understood to have been altogether mine, from which the greater part of the merit (if any there was in contending against a whole army for the space of four hours) is taken away from me. To elucidate this matter it appears necessary I should state that when it was reported on the 21st – at Chateauguay church, at night, the enemy had surprised the picket at Pepper's (Piper's) Road I was desired to move with my corps to the English River and finding when there that the enemy's intention appeared to move down the River Chateauguay on his way to Montreal, I lost no time in pushing on the troops and took up three advanced positions and began to fortify them as well as I could (having then only few axes) and distributed the troops for their defense. I ordered also the famous abbatis, situated two miles in front of the above stated positions to which I marched on the 26th, from which I reconnoitered the American army in the act of advance: from which I completed my dispositions for the defense of both sides of the Chateauguay; from whence after an obstinate engagement of four hours I succeeded in defeating their project of penetrating in the country and finally obliged him to retire to his former position five miles back with the loss of about 70 killed and 16 prisoners besides a great quantity of wounded, about 150 stand of arms and six drums which fell into our hands. Moreover he has retired into his own country.

It is true Gen. de Watteville inspected my positions and approved of them and of the orders I had given for their defense. The dispositions to receive the enemy on the 26th were made by myself; no one interfered with them and no officer of superior rank came up until the action was over. It is true that I was ably seconded by Lt. Col. McDonall [sic] of the Glengarry Fencibles, who had taken up a 4th position two days before the action, and by all the officers under my command – I regret to observe that in perusing the order of the 27th that it is supposed that I had been thrown forward to cover working parties. The idea is erroneous insomuch as there were no works carrying on there but such abbatis and defenses as appeared to me necessary to prevent my positions from being outflanked or forced; those I ordered myself, no engineer directed them. I placed myself in front of the abbatis with the view to begin the defense of the country. I judged it a good position from whence I could have a good view of the enemy's columns, which I was apprized were in full march. This I did of my own accord. It was a desperate undertaking. It succeeded and the enemy instead of going to Montreal is gone to Four Corners. The enemy's intentions are ascertained by concurring circumstances and by the report of prisoners. He was not then in full march with all his baggage and artillery for the purpose of attacking a few workmen.

These are the true circumstances attending the action of the 26th and it grieves me to the heart to see that I must share the merit of the action and that it must be reduced to my having covered a few

piquet duty

workmen. Methinks if any merit is to be obtained, I am entitled to the whole.

I cannot conclude without soliciting that this representation may be laid before his Excellency the Governor-General to whose justice I confidently appeal.

> I have the honor to be
> Sir,
> Your most obedient
> Humble servant
> (signed) Chl: deSalaberry
> Lt. Col. Com. of Voltigeurs

There were too many prominent Canadian families represented on the battlefield of Chateauguay to allow Prevost's misrepresentations to go unchallenged. The general public received their information through a detailed report published in the *Gazette* a few days after the battle and signed by *Témoin Oculaire*.[2]

In his own straightforward way wrote de Salaberry: "Prevost is trying to do everything that he can to tarnish the little glory that I have gained".[3] Others were much more animated. The Honorable Juchereau Duchesnay whose father and uncle were present at the battle, remarked that:

> It is difficult which to admire the more – his personal courage as an individual or his skill and talents as a commander.[4]

When he saw the General Orders after the battle, d'Aubreville, who was Quartermaster in de Watteville's Regiment, wrote to de Salaberry:

> My wishes will not be completely satisfied until your virtues, your talent and your services will have been recompensed in a most fitting way and until we can unanimously claim that we have given justice to the Hero of Chateauguay.[5]

The Duke of Kent himself wrote to Louis de Salaberry a few months later (15 March 1814):

104

I saw with dismay that the report made by the Adjutant-General did not render him [Charles] sufficient justice . . . . Over here everyone attributes to him all the honour and looks to him as the hero who saved the province of Lower Canada . . . . I have also spoken about this with the Duke of York who appears perfectly convinced that it is to your son that we owe it all.[6]

Colonial Secretary Bathurst's reply to Prevost's report indicated that no one had really been fooled:

His Royal Highness has observed with the greatest satisfaction the skill and gallantry so conspicuously displayed by the officers and men who composed the detachment of troops opposed to General Hampton's army. By the resistance which they successfully made to the enemy, so vastly disproportionate, the confidence of the enemy has been lowered, their plans disconcerted and the safety of that part of the Canadian frontier ensured. It gives His Royal Highness peculiar pleasure to find that His Majesty's Canadian subjects have had the opportunity (which His Royal Highness has long been desirous should be afforded them) of disproving by their own brilliant exertions in defence of their country that calumnious charge of disaffection and disloyalty with which the enemy prefaced his first invasion of the province. *To Colonel de Salaberry in particular, and to all the officers under his command in general, you will not fail to express His Royal Highness' most gracious approbation of their meritorious and most distinguished services.*[7]

Campaigning in the Fall

While these letters, reports, and General Orders went back and forth, the war continued. De Salaberry was seriously concerned about the health and well-being of his men: they had been on the move constantly since Hampton's first initiatives in September. They had made several forced marches, fought several serious battles, and

105

arms drill

their uniforms were tattered and worn from their work in the dense forests and swamps. By late November many of the men had been weakened by sickness and exposure. They were close to being a spent force.

However, on 23 November Prevost ordered de Salaberry to attack the enemy camp at Four Corners with about 300 men. It was another hopeless venture, but by 3 p.m., two hours later than he had planned, de Salaberry had his men on the march.

For eight kilometres they ploughed through mud and water up to their knees. He had to order the dragoons back because their horses were not rough shod and were frequently slipping and falling on the treacherous road. By nightfall the force was about halfway to its objective, having covered about 25 kilometres. De Salaberry found a small elevated spot in the woods and gathered the men together to spend the night. They were a sorry-looking lot as they filed into their bivouac. The men were soaked through from the rain that started around 6 p.m., and their condition was not improved by a frost that night. As they huddled together, restless and uncomfortable, de Salaberry sent Captains Milnes and Barron ahead to the lines to gather intelligence; they were to report to him during the night near Elliot's Mills.

That night there was no word from Captain Milnes. The road ahead was worse than the part they had already come through, so de Salaberry refused to commit his men to a line of march until he had some intelligence of the enemy. It was a frustrating wait through the next day, but only two men deserted. Finally, de Salaberry called a council of war with his officers.

As they saw it the situation bordered on the ridiculous. It was far too late in the season and the weather too severe to be practical for a campaign. They could not keep their men in any kind of fighting trim while they camped in swamps and were exposed to a combination of heavy rains and severe frosts. There were no houses or possible refuges in that part of the country. What worried de Salaberry most of all was the fact that even if they did advance and fight a battle, they would have to return whether they won or lost; the men would be in even worse condition to face that march. Many of their wounded would be lost on the trek through the uninhabited bush and swamp.

Still, there was no word from Captain Milnes. De Salaberry could assume only that he was a prisoner. Captain Barron reported back that the Americans had two pieces of heavy artillery and dragoons, but he had received his information from an informant rather than from observation and his report could not be relied upon. De Salaberry then sent out one of his own men, Captain Ecuyer, to scout the American camp.

Ecuyer returned with a report that the American strength was between 800 and 900 men and that they had two 24-pounders and cavalry. This was obviously too strong a camp for a force the size and condition of de Salaberry's to defeat. He turned the men around and led them back to their own base camp.

This campaign and others like it in swamps and bad weather gave de Salaberry the rheumatism that plagued him for the rest of his life.

De Salaberry's Health Deteriorates

In January de Salaberry was granted a short furlough with his wife in Montreal. He was so crippled with fevers and rheumatism that he considered retiring from active service. He wrote to his father on 24 January 1814:

> You see, it is determined I can not rest a moment, I can not long stand this or I shall be killed. I am very harassed and my constitution much injured. I must put an end to these miseries.[8]

A week later he was called from his sickbed at midnight when a dispatch rider arrived with orders for him to march immediately to Coteau-du-Lac. It was feared that the American, Scott, would attack there from French Mills on the Salmon River. De Salaberry quickly put together a force of about 600 men with his own Voltigeurs and four companies of the 49th Regiment. It was a long cold march of about 65 kilometres up the St Lawrence

Valley and, in the bitter weather, 30 men were lost to frostbite.

Scott's attack did not materialize; it had been just another of the rumours that are so common in wartime. As soon as he verified that it had been a false alarm, de Salaberry marched his men back to Montreal, where he arrived on 4 February sicker than ever.

Accolades

The early winter held some pleasant interludes for de Salaberry. In January, the Legislative Assembly unanimously passed a vote of thanks to him for the victory at Chateauguay. A copy of this resolution reached him at Coteau-du-Lac along with a note from the Speaker of the Assembly, A. Panet, who added his personal feelings:

> Although I participated as a member of the Assembly in the unanimous approbation of your conduct, permit me to express the great satisfaction I experienced individually on the occasion, ...[9]

The resolution, itself, which was passed on 25 January 1814 read:

> Resolved, unanimously, that the thanks of this Assembly be given to Lieutenant Colonel Charles de Salaberry, commander of the Canadian Voltigeurs, and to the other officers under his command, for their distinguished efforts in the glorious action which took place on Tuesday, the twenty-sixth day of October last, on the Chateauguay river; and that the Speaker of this Assembly be charged with communicating them to the above mentioned Lieutenant Colonel Charles de Salaberry and to the various other officers – that this Assembly deeply appreciates the distinguished valour and discipline shown by the non-commissioned officers, soldiers and militiamen of the little band under the immediate command of Lieutenant Colonel Charles de Salaberry, in the memorable defeat of the American army under the command of General Hampton at the above-mentioned

110

The Military General Service Medal with the Bar for the Battle of Chateauguay.

Chateauguay, and that these be communicated to them by the officers commanding those units, who are asked to thank them for their courageous and exemplary conduct.[10]

The courier with these messages reached Coteau-du-Lac on 31 January; de Salaberry responded immediately:

I received today the resolution that you did me the honour to send on behalf of the Honourable *Chambre d'Assemblée*, by which that respectable body deigns to offer its thanks to me and to all the fighting men under my command at the action of Chateauguay.

When my three hundred brave companions thwarted the enemy army from penetrating into the country, we only thought, they and I, of simply doing our duty, serving our sovereign and saving our country from the miseries of an invasion. In the single satisfaction of having succeeded, we found ample reward: however today we have received another and highly esteemed one in the distinguished honour which it has pleased the *Chambre d'Assemblée* to confer on us. It offers us its thanks. This generous gesture has made a very lively and profound impression on us which will last for the rest of our lives. The country shows itself, through its representatives, nobly grateful, putting the highest price and the most flattering, on the services of its subjects.

We wish to express our most complete and respectful thanks. May the Honourable Assembly deign to accept it as our constant sentiment . . . .

According to the wishes of the Assembly their resolutions will be communicated accurately and as quickly as possible to the officers, non-commissioned officers and the brave men of all ranks who took part in the action of October 26th last.[11]

The following month, the Upper House (Legislative Council) passed a similar resolution.

In the popular press, a poet by the name of Joseph Mermet published *La Victoire de Chateauguay*.[12] The poem

112

was in the heroic mode: it likened de Salaberry to Leonidas and Chateauguay to the famous Thermopylae. The nickname, Leonidas, caught the popular imagination and Mermet, a Lieutenant in de Watteville's regiment, became an idol of Canadian salons.

During February 1814 de Salaberry's health improved somewhat, but the years of campaigning had taken their toll. The fevers and sickness of the West Indies and Walcharen made his recovery a slow one.

It was with considerable relief, therefore, that in late February he accepted a new appointment as Inspecting Field Officer. This was more a lateral transfer than a promotion, and there was no appreciable increase in salary. But it did reduce the amount of front line campaigning that he would have to do. It also involved some major changes for the *Voltigeurs*. Major Herriot, who had commanded the Voltigeur companies in Upper Canada, assumed the command of the regiment; Chevalier Duchesnay became second-in-command. Two weeks later, the Canadian Chasseurs were brigaded with the Voltigeurs under de Salaberry's superintendence.

The officers of the Voltigeurs wanted very much to give de Salaberry a memento from the regiment and asked whether he would prefer a sword or a silver plate. De Salaberry suggested that he would prefer the plate because it would be something that could more easily be handed down in the family. The actual presentation took place on St Patrick's Day, 1814, in Montreal. The message of presentation read:

> Sir
>
> Representing the officers of the Canadian Voltigeurs, we beg leave in their names and our own to present you with a piece of plate as a trifling mark of the esteem we entertain for you as a friend and more particularly for the services you have rendered us and the corps at large in your continued assiduity and universal attention to the well-disciplining and internal management thereof whilst under your command.
>
> Permit us to express our sincere regret at your departure from amongst us, at the same time we feel

most truly gratified at your promotion, more particularly from the nature thereof. We flatter ourselves it will not deprive us entirely of the advantages we may derive from your personal attention to the interest of the corps.

We have the honor to remain
Sir
Your most obed and Humble servant
signed/Fred Herriot Major C.V.
Benj. Ecuyer Capt C.V.
Thos. Plase Paymaster

The piece of plate was a soup tureen and it bears the inscription:

Presented
To Lieut. Colonel Charles de Salaberry by the
officers of the
Canadian Voltigeurs
As a token of their personal esteem for his private
character
as a proof of their gratitude for his spirit of justice
and
correct discipline while Lieut. Colonel, commanding
their corps
and
as a feeble testimony
of the high sense which they entertain of the coolness
and
intrepidity so often displayed by him in the field
but more
particularly in the action of the 26th of October 1813
at Chateauguay

New Threats

The Americans launched another invasion down the Richelieu Valley in March 1814. Major-General Wilkinson commanded an army of about 2,000 men including three brigades of regular infantry, a squadron of cavalry, and eight guns. They took Odelltown and, using it as a base of operation, they moved on downriver.

The British piquets on the road to Burtonville were driven in and the Americans moved on to the next outpost, the mill in Lacolle. The small garrison there grimly held firm while the Americans pounded away at the mill with an 18-pounder, trying to open a breach in the wall.

When word of the American advance reached the British base at Burtonville, a company of Voltigeurs and one of the Fencibles were immediately ordered out to support the beleaguered garrison at Lacolle. The roads were flooded in several places, and the relief column was forced at times to wade through icy, waist-deep water.

When the reinforcements arrived, the garrison sallied out and together the two forces charged the Americans in the hope of capturing the gun. It was a brave move against a strong position, and the Americans fell back except for one man. He waited by the gun until the British were only a pace or two away and then he fired it. The Americans now took heart and began firing on the flanks of the small force and driving them back.

The threat posed by the presence of Wilkinson's army on Canadian soil brought de Salaberry back to the field. Early in April he brought together a force of about 800 men at l'Acadie to challenge this new invasion. Moving south, he drove the Americans before him. When he reached Wilkinson's base at Odelltown, he found that they had pulled out and retired on the road to Plattsburg.

Wilkinson and a number of other senior American generals were now replaced by younger and abler officers. George Izard, who had been Hampton's second-in-command at Chateauguay, was now a major-general. He was given command of the frontier in the area of Lake Champlain with about 6,000 men. Izard was a much more considerable threat than Wilkinson had been. Instead of basing his army in Plattsburg as his predecessor had done, he moved forward and entrenched it at Champlain just a kilometre or two inside the American border and about seven kilometres from Odelltown.

The British responded in July by sending de Salaberry with about 2,200 men and some artillery to take up a position at Odelltown – in effect, to keep Izard in the United States. During the summer Izard frequently sent raiding parties across the border to probe de Salaberry's strength and keep his force on the *qui vive*. The Voltigeurs spent the summer quartered in bark cabins in the area, and took a major role in the skirmishes with these raiding parties. The Voltigeurs were invariably successful in driving the Americans back across the border. Although these actions normally involved relatively small numbers of men, some of them were hotly contested battles.

Chapter Nine

The End of A Military Career

The Plattsburg Campaign

During July and August British reinforcements arrived in Quebec. Wellington's campaign in the Spanish Peninsula had been completed successfully and 16,000 of his veterans sailed to Canada.

Prevost lost no time. Quickly, he put together an army of 11,000 men to destroy the American naval establishment at Plattsburg. He planned it as a combined operation with the small British squadron on Lake Champlain and personally took command of the army. The Voltigeurs joined Wellington's veterans for this campaign.

Prevost marched slowly up the Richelieu and crossed the border on 1 September. He established his army around the outskirts of Plattsburg by the sixth. Brigadier General Macomb commanded the defences of Plattsburg with a force of about 1,500 regulars and 1,800 militia against Prevost's 11,000 veterans.

Captain George Downie commanded the British squadron. He did not favour Prevost's pressure for a naval assault because the squadron was far from ready. In fact, his gun crews were only filled as he prepared to sail into battle so that they had little time to practice together. The real danger for the squadron would be if it had to fight the American fleet in its anchorage at Plattsburg Bay where the Americans were protected by the shore batteries.

Downie felt that if Prevost were able to take the shore batteries, the Americans would be forced to sail into open water to escape having their own batteries turned on them. In open water the British would have, at least, a fighting chance.

117

Prevost determined to storm the batteries at the moment Downie engaged the American fleet. On 11 September Downie signalled his move to Prevost by scaling (firing cartridges without shot) his guns, and sailed into battle. Prevost responded by delaying his assault on the batteries. In fact, when he finally permitted the troops to start moving forward, they did not know which roads to follow. Prevost had been on the site for five days and had made no effort to gather intelligence of either the strength of the enemy or the terrain he would have to cross.

Without the planned support of Prevost's land forces, the British squadron took a severe pounding and Downie himself was killed. When the flags on the battered ships were finally hauled down, Prevost ordered his troops, who had just begun to advance, to pull back. He destroyed his surplus stores and marched his men back to Canada. He lost more men through desertion on the return march than had been lost in the fighting. The British veterans were disgusted and humiliated. They knew that Plattsburg could not have survived more than half an hour if they had been free to attack.

De Salaberry Retires from the Army

During the summer de Salaberry had been giving much thought to his own future. He was pretty well convinced that he should retire from active service. The Duke of Kent was pressuring him to stay in the army as long as there was no likelihood of his being transferred out of Canada. He was trying to get de Salaberry nominated as an honorary aide-de-camp to the Prince Regent, a position which would bring a promotion to full colonel. As a colonel he could then become Colonel Propriétaire of the Canadian Regiment.

But de Salaberry was well aware that further promotion was extremely unlikely for a Catholic in the British army. The traditional anti-Catholic sentiment and fear of popery in Britain had declined sufficiently to permit Catholic officers to occasionally rise to the rank of Lieutenant-Colonel, but all the more senior ranks were generally reserved for members of the official Church of England. His family was also concerned because whenever he led his men into battle, he made a point of exposing himself to enemy fire in order to inspire his men.

After the Plattsburg campaign there was little activity on his front. He obtained a furlough on 17 September 1814 to seriously consider the matter of retirement. The war would certainly not last much longer and he was determined to remain in Canada. On 18 November he applied for retirement on half pay.

The Treaty of Ghent was signed on Christmas Eve 1814, and the war was officially over. On 1 March 1815 a General Order was posted formally disbanding the Voltigeurs as of 15 March. The officers were put on half pay – just as if they had been in a regular British regiment. At the same time, de Salaberry's half pay retirement came through. In effect, this was accomplished by his transferring as Lieutenant Colonel from the 60th Regiment to the Supply Corps Volunteers, Canada.

The Legislative Assembly tried to obtain a grant of Crown Land for him by petitioning both Prevost and the Prince Regent. They suggested that this kind of recognition would clearly demonstrate the Crown's appreciation of the role of the colonists in the defense of the colony, and would encourage others to do likewise in the future.

The Crown was unwilling to make the land grant, but it had a special gold medal struck to commemorate the Battle of Chateauguay and sent it to de Salaberry with this covering letter:

Horse Guards
1st July 1815.

Sir,

The Prince Regent having been graciously pleased to command, in the name and on behalf of His Majesty, that you should be permitted to bear a Medal commemorative of the Battle of Chateauguay, I have the satisfaction to transmit to you the Medal, which, with the Approbation of His Royal Highness, has been struck for the occasion, and to desire that you acknowledge the receipt of it.

I am,

Sir,
Your's
Frederick[1]

The medal itself showed Britannia on the obverse, her left hand holding a palm and her right crowning a British lion at her feet. The reverse bore the legend "Chateauguay".[2]

On the centenary of the battle, in 1913, the writer and a great grandson of de Salaberry, de Roquebrune commented with some exasperation:

Charles saved a vast country (at Chateauguay) for England; Louis XIV would have made him a rich man; Napoleon would have made him a prince; the English king gave him a medal.[3]

Lieutenant Colonel Macdonell, who had commanded the reserves at Chateauguay, retired to England at the end of the war. Frustrated with the way that the British government chose to overlook the outstanding services of some of her officers, he spoke to Kent about proper recognition for de Salaberry. The Duke advised him to draft an official communique so that he could use it as evidence to counterbalance the official report of Prevost.

On 14 January 1817, Macdonell submitted his report:

Having been second in command in the important action of Chateauguai [sic] in Lower Canada, I can pledge my honour that the merit of occupying that position and of fighting that action is exclusively due to Lieutenant Colonel de Salaberry who acted in both respects entirely from his own judgement – Major-General de Watteville having come up from his station some miles in the rear at the close of that affair after the enemy had been defeated, in consequence of a notification sent to him by myself that we were then warmly engaged with the enemy.

120

De Salaberry's medal of the Order of the Bath.

Lieutenant Colonel de Salaberry having in this affair had the good fortune to defeat a division of 7,000 regular troops, the largest regular army that the American nation has ever yet brought into action; I hope H.R.H. the Commander-in-Chief will do him the honour to take the subject into his gracious consideration.[4]

De Watteville had kept a discreet silence during Prevost's attempt to discredit de Salaberry. But his journals, which are still in his family's archives in Switzerland, substantiate in detail what de Salaberry and, later, Macdonell, claimed as the correct sequence of events. In his journal entry for 26 October 1813, he recorded that he and Prevost were on a tour of various military positions when a dispatch rider brought the word of the American attack. Turning their horses, they rode to the battlefield and arrived after all the fighting had ceased on both sides of the river.

This evidence was not available at the time, but Macdonell's testimony did have some effect. In the Army List of 1818 both he and de Salaberry were honoured by being created Companions of the Order of the Bath.

De Salaberry's manor house at Chambly as it appears today.

Chapter Ten

De Salaberry in Public Life

Politics

De Salaberry was 36 when he retired from the army. He approached with enthusiasm his new full-time role as Seigneur of Chambly. He also completed his manor house, an impressive stone building on the shore of the Richelieu River close to Fort Chambly.

In 1815, he was asked by a committee from Bedford County to be a candidate for the Legislative Assembly. Politics was not one of de Salaberry's major interests, but he agreed to serve if elected. He made it clear that he would not actively campaign for himself. The election got underway on 3 December, but it was annulled when his opponent, McCord, challenged it on a technicality. The second election was scheduled for January, but de Salaberry had had enough of the petty bickering and withdrew in order to concentrate on things of more immediate interest to him.

One of the ideas that caught his imagination was the possibility of building a canal around the rapids in the Richelieu between Chambly and St-Jean. As early as December 1815, he had drafted a tentative plan for the route it could follow, and was considering forming a company to build it. The canal would open a water route from the St Lawrence to Lake Champlain, and there connect with the route down the Hudson River. It would provide a more economical mode of transportation for the bountiful farm produce of the region which came to be known as "the granary of Lower Canada".

The active part de Salaberry took in advocating the canal to both the public and the Legislative Assembly led to his appointment as Commissioner of Interior Communication for Kent County and, finally, on 1 April 1818, to government approval for the formation of a canal company. It was called Proprietors of Chambly Canal and was given the authority to undertake construction.

Political and financial setbacks delayed the beginning of construction until 1829, and the canal was not completed until 1843. Unfortunately de Salaberry died before he saw his dream fulfilled. The canal was a significant economic resource until the First World War. It is now under the jurisdiction of Parks Canada, and fills an important cultural and recreational role in the historic Richelieu Valley.

The Union Bill Controversy

De Salaberry's own fortunes improved a little in 1816. He inherited, through his wife's family, the seigneurial lands of Beaulac and Dodsgand. The revenues from these farms, as well as from his own farm and mill, finally removed from him the burden of financial worry, although he was by no means wealthy.

Two years later, his father-in-law died and de Salaberry was chosen to replace him in the Legislative Council. This was a little out of the ordinary since his own father, Louis, was already a member; normally only one member of a family was permitted on the Council. Actually, Charles saw this appointment largely as an honorary one and, after the first year during which he attended sessions regularly, he normally stayed away.

Political problems that had been plaguing Upper and Lower Canada since the war suddenly became critical issues. Word was received in 1822 that the British government was considering a bill for the union of the two Canadas. One of the principal objectives of this was the reduction of the French-Canadian majority in the Assembly of Lower Canada. They were not enthusiastic supporters of measures that the merchants felt were essential to the economic growth of the colony. The French-Canadians were alarmed and angry at the prospect. De Salaberry took his place in the Legislative Council in order to fight any such move. A motion in favor of union was defeated, but it soon became apparent that its opponents had insufficient strength in that body to have any serious impact. Both Charles and his father resigned their seats in order to actively campaign against the Union Bill.

Public reaction to the bill reached the grass roots; Anti-Union Committees were organized in all the parishes. Louis de Salaberry was selected president of the one in Quebec City, and Charles was a member of the one formed in Montreal. His colleagues on the Montreal committee were such notable citizens as Louis Guy, Charles de St Ours, P.D. Debartzch, L.R. Chaussegros de Léry, Louis Joseph Papineau, Denis Benjamin Viger, Joseph Bédard, Augustin Cuvillier and Louis Bourdages. The committees circulated petitions, and finally decided to take their case to London in 1823. Charles de Salaberry was asked to be one of the two delegates, but he felt that his health would be unequal to the task. He recommended that Louis Joseph Papineau go in his place. Papineau was able to generate opposition to the bill and to delay its enactment.

Social Life

Throughout this troubled political period, private and social life continued. In fact, de Salaberry was almost ruined in November 1823 when a stove overheated in one of his estate's outbuildings.

It was a desperate situation: the outbuildings were ablaze, the mill was gone, and the flames were edging dangerously close to the house. Everyone turned out to help and the fire was finally contained and the house saved. There had been serious financial loss but, in the best tradition of early settlements, de Salaberry was able to count his blessings in the smoke-begrimed neighbours and friends who had turned out to help him when he needed them so badly.

Jacques Viger and his wife, Marie, were close friends of the de Salaberry's. Jacques was an ardent antiquarian, and his passion for recording events and preserving documents has been a blessing for generations of historians.

Later (in 1833) he became the first mayor of Montreal. Marie Viger stood up as godmother for de Salaberry's daughter, Catherine, on 12 September 1825, and later that month she and Charles were part of an impressive ceremony in Montreal. The chapel of St James Cathedral[1] at Dominion Square was blessed and opened to the public by Bishop Lartique on 18 September. Three days later, the first bell was christened and lifted to its place in the belfry. Marie Viger and Charles de Salaberry were the symbolic godparents for this bell. It was named Marie Charles in their honour.

Death of de Salaberry

Jacques Viger had been working on a project to help immortalize his friend and former commanding officer. He wrote to His Excellency Sir F.N. Burton, the Lieutenant Governor of Quebec, asking him to be the patron of a subscription campaign across the province for a gravure (a print made from an engraving) of Charles, "whose name already belongs to history".[2] Burton ordered six copies but declined the patronship with the suggestion that the office be filled by a military man. The campaign met with some success and there is a record of one order from a Louis Willcocks for 500 of the pictures.[3]

The original miniature of the gravure was the work of a New York artist, Anson Dickinson, and the engraving from it was done by A.B. Durand. When de Salaberry was asked for his impression of the picture, he replied good humouredly, "I think, as do a lot of others, that the darn nose is a little too big."[4] Notwithstanding this criticism, it was selected to be shown at an art exhibit in New York in 1826.

No longer in the army, no longer in politics, de Salaberry now spent most of his time among his friends and his family in and around Chambly. It was not as quiet a time as one might imagine. There was an estate to run, and the whole social interaction of a dispersed rural community in which to participate. Charles joined in the local parties not as the renowned military hero, but as a neighbour – sometimes as guest and often as host.

Charles de Salaberry as he appeared in the Durand engraving.

It was during such a party on the evening of 26 February 1829 in the home of his friend, Mr Hatte, that tragedy struck. In the midst of a conversation with his host, Charles paled, excused himself, and quickly withdrew, only to collapse with apoplexy.

His wife, Marie-Anne, had him carried home carefully. The doctor tried to bring him around, even bled him twice, but it was to no avail. Early the next morning he regained all his faculties except that of speech. Surrounded by his family, one of Canada's great military heroes died peacefully at the age of only 51. His body was laid to rest near the shore of the Richelieu River, in the church yard at Chambly. The plain stone that marks his grave is not particularly different from others in that little cemetery and its epitaph is quite simple:

Erige
A La Memoire De L'honorable
Charles Michel D'yrumberry
De Salaberry.C.B.
Le Hero De Chateauguay
Le Leonidas Canadien
Decede a Chambly
Le 27 Fevrier 1829
Age De 51 Ans

Chapter Eleven

The Tradition Carries On

The Family

When he died, de Salaberry left behind a family that had a rough road ahead of it. Marie-Anne-Julie was 42 years old and had seven children to bring up: Alphonse, who was almost sixteen, Hermine (thirteen), Charlotte (eleven), Louis-Michel (ten), René (eight), Maurice (four), and Catherine (three). The pension that she received from the government was too small to be much help. She carried on with dogged determination and the help of family and friends.

The youngest daughter, Catherine, was only six years old when she died of cholera in 1832. Five years later, Maurice, who was then 13, suffered a fatal hunting accident and became the third de Salaberry in the little cemetery behind the parish church of Chambly. Charles' second, Louis-Michel, did not marry and died of cancer in 1870.

Both of the daughters married at the age of 21: Marie-Anne-Hermine to Doctor Jacob Glen in 1836, and Charlotte-Emelie to Augustus Hatt in 1838. Hermine lost her husband in 1837 after only 15 months of marriage, and she herself died in 1844. Her sister had nine children and lived to the age of 79.

Alphonse

The oldest son, Alphonse, was offered a commission in the army in 1830, but his mother felt that the family had suffered sufficiently from military careers and the offer was refused.

131

He was called to the Legislative Council in 1837. Before he could take his seat, rebellion had broken out and the constitution was suspended. During the rebellion, he played a very mature role in maintaining the family's traditional loyalty to legitimate government without losing his perspective on the frustrations and fears that led some of his neighbours to take up arms against that government.

When word was brought to him that rebels or patriotes were planning to fortify themselves in the ruins of nearby Fort Chambly, Alphonse quickly organized a force of about 30 volunteers and moved into the old fort. As he had foreseen, the patriote force had been more inclined to occupy the fort as a gesture and a challenge than to actually offer battle, and his quick manoeuvre defused the situation. In an effort to further restore peace, he negotiated with Governor Sir John Colborne an amnesty for the patriotes who voluntarily laid down their arms.

In 1839 he received the largely honorary post of aide-de-camp, which involved accompanying the governor on State occasions. Two years later he ran for election to the Assembly for Rouville County. He won the seat but sat for only one session. He took up law and, in 1845, was admitted to the bar in Montreal. He went into practice there with R.S.M. Bouchette. In 1846 he married Marie-Emelie Guy in Montreal. They had eight children, three girls and five boys. Only three of the boys and two of the girls survived childhood, and none of the boys married.

In 1847 he was named Coroner of Montreal (co-jointly with Joseph Jones) and in the following year was appointed Deputy Adjutant-General of the militia of Lower Canada. It is interesting to note that the Adjutant-General was his father's former commanding officer, de Rottenburg.

Although he was a big, strong man like his father, Alphonse suffered from a heart condition. In 1867, at the age of 53, he suffered a fatal heart attack. He was buried with full military honours in the churchyard at Beauport.[1]

De Salaberry's tombstone in the churchyard at Chambly.

René

The family name was carried on through the third surviving son, Charles-René-Leonidas. Quick tempered and impetuous, with the build and strength of his father, he was a young man to be reckoned with.

He married at the age of 28 and settled down at St Mathias de Rouville with his wife, Marie-Victorine-Cordelia Franchere. His mother came to live with them and, together with the two children, Leonidas-Charles (born 1849) and Lilia (born 1851) they were a happy family. The arrival of a third child in 1853 seemed to bring only more happiness, but five months later (25 January 1854) the baby died. Just three months after this, René was shaken when his wife died and, the following day, his mother.

His whole life in Lower Canada seemed to have fallen apart. One of his wife's sisters took the two children and raised them at her manor house at L'Assomption, and René joined the Hudson Bay Company as an engineer in the northwest.

For five years (1855-1860) he travelled throughout that area, often in company with the famous missionary, Father Lacombe. He made friends with a number of Indian leaders and learned some of their languages. In later years, Indian leaders visiting Ottawa would travel to Chambly to visit their friend René de Salaberry.

When René returned from the northwest in the spring of 1860, he involved himself a great deal in militia affairs, particularly with the 9th Voltigeurs of Quebec, of which he had been the founding Lieutenant Colonel in 1851.

In 1869 he was appointed Superintendant of Forests for the Montreal District. His personal life also took a turn for the better: he fell in love and remarried. His second wife was Louise-Josephine Allard of Chambly. The couple took up residence there.

A few months later, the federal government of John A. Macdonald was faced with the Red River Rebellion. It chose a commission of three men who knew the area and the people well to go to Fort Garry and negotiate with the Métis who were rebelling against the apparent loss of their farms. The commission was made up of Grand

René de Salaberry, Charles' third and surviving son.

Vicar Thibeault, Donald A. Smith (later Lord Strathcona) and Colonel de Salaberry. Although they had some initial success, the situation had already gone too far to be settled by negotiation. For a time they were imprisoned by Louis Riel.

When de Salaberry returned to Chambly, he began to raise a second family. René was born in 1870, Alice in 1872, and Thérèse in 1874. A fourth child, Pierre, born in 1876, lived for only three days. The following year tragedy struck again when René's wife sickened and died. René was grief-stricken, but he raised the three children. He was particularly dedicated to instilling in them a strong sense of their heritage.

The two children of his first marriage continued to live with their aunt, but were still very much a part of René's family. When relatives from France came to visit, Charles stayed with his father for the entire visit in order to learn more about the family. Years later, when René was extremely ill, it was Lilia he went to live with and who cared for him until his death.

In 1880 the children of his second marriage were sent to school in Montreal. Also in this year René married for a third time. His wife was Marie-Louise Baby, sister of the well known Judge Baby. René was 60 years old at this time. He died two years later without having any children from the third marriage.

Both his sons (one from each of his first two marriages) became lawyers. The older one went to practice in the United States, where he married but had no children.

To this day, the family name is continued through the descendants of René.

Epitaph

From time to time people who are aware of his exploits have undertaken projects to commemorate Charles Michel d'Irumberry de Salaberry and his heroics at Chateauguay. Throughout the Montreal and Richelieu valley areas one frequently finds streets named for de Salaberry, the

Philippe Hébert's statue of de Salaberry in Chambly.

Voltigeurs, and Chateauguay. Parks, islands, subdivisions, buildings and a Regiment have all been named in his honour.

The earliest effort to commemorate de Salaberry after his death was undertaken by J.O. Dion, a fervent patriot, who wanted a monument of the man erected in Chambly. He first proposed the idea in 1870, but it took a decade of writing letters, giving speeches, and practically begging from door to door in numerous towns and villages before his dream could be realized. The monument was finally unveiled on 7 June 1881 by the Marquess of Lorne, Governor-General of Canada.

It was the work of Philippe Hébert and was, in fact, the first such monument by a Canadian sculptor. He had used René, de Salaberry's son, as his model for the physique of his subject, and placed his work on a stone plinth so that the overall height reaches a little over eight metres.

Another statue to de Salaberry was erected in September 1894 in a niche in the facade of the Parliament Buildings in Quebec City. It too is the work of Philippe Hébert and shows the subject in an action pose with a drawn sabre. Other statues in the series include ones of Montcalm, Wolfe, and Frontenac.[2]

The site of the battle of Chateauguay itself was marked with a granite obelisk in 1895. Much more recently, in the late 1970s, Parks Canada, the federal government agency responsible for National Historic Sites, opened an interpretation centre and site museum near the battlefield. It exhibits a fine collection of material relating to de Salaberry and the battle.

L'Envoi

Charles Michel d'Irumberry de Salaberry, soldier of the Empire/defender of Quebec, inherited a proud and demanding legacy; he lived up to it; added to it; and passed it on.

The granite obelisk erected in 1895 to mark the site of the Battle of Chateauguay.

Appendix A

De Salaberry's letter to his father after the Battle of Chateauguay.

Dans le bois en haut de la rivière
Chateauguay, Oct. 29, 1813

My dear Father,

The 26th has been a glorious day for me and those of my troops engaged. The American army commanded by Gen'l. Hampton and another general has been repulsed by a little band – all Canadians – and yesterday that army commenced its retreat, or will endeavour to get into this country through some other road. The enemy's force consisted of all his troops, about 7,000 men and 5 pieces of cannon, 300 cavalry. The action lasted four hours, and it ended in the enemy being obliged to return to his former position five miles back, leaving many of his dead and wounded behind and a great number of his men scattered in the woods, also many drums, 150 Firelocks and baggage. The number of my men engaged did not exceed three hundred. The rest were in reserve in the lines I had constructed. Our killed and wounded were only 24 including officers, there were none but Canadians amongst us. I was in the first line during the whole of the action and afterwards, with a small reserve, beat off a large body of Americans and saved Capt. Daily and his company. I chose my own ground and after the action pushed in my piquets two miles in advance of where they were before. Without arrogating to myself too much credit, I am proud to think that this defence, on our part, has at least prevented the American army from penetrating to La Prairie. We are here situated about 35 miles from

Montreal. This is certainly a most extraordinary affair. Chevalier and all officers in this action conducted themselves with great bravery. The prisoners have been about 25. We are all very much harassed and I am not well.

I remain in haste,
my dear Father, Yours faithfully
Ch. de Salaberry

Appendix B

Letter from Panet (Speaker of the Assembly) and copy of the Assembly's Vote of Thanks.

Quebec, 25th January 1814

Sir,

    In obedience to the commands of the House of Assembly of Lower Canada I have the honor to inclose you one of their Resolutions dated the 25th january 1814.

    Although I participated as a member of the Assembly in the unanimous approbation of your conduct, permit me to express the great satisfaction I experienced individually on the occasion, and to assure you that I am,

Sir
Your obedient and
very humble servant,
A. Panet
Speaker

To
Lieut-Colonel de Salaberry
  Canadian Voltigeurs.

Province du Bas Canada
Chambre d'Assemblée
Mardi, 25 janvier 1814,

Résolu, nemine contradicente, que les remerciements de cette Chambre soient donnés au lieutenant-colonel Charles de Salaberry, commandant des Voltigeurs Canadiens, et aux différents autres officiers sous son commandement, pour leurs efforts distingués dans l'affaire glorieuse qui a eu lieu mardi le vingt-sixième jour d'octobre dernier, sur la rivière Châteauguay; et que l'orateur de cette Chambre soit chargé de les signifier au dit lieutenant-colonel Charles de Salaberry et aux différents autres officiers – que cette Chambre reconnait sensiblement la valeur distinguée et la discipline qu'ont montrées les officiers non commissionnés, soldats et miliciens de la petite bande sous le commandement immédiat du lieutenant-colonel Charles de Salaberry, dans la défaite signalée de l'armée américaine sous le commandement du général Hampton à Châteauguay susdit, et qu'ils leur soient signifiés par les officiers commandants de ces corps, qui sont priés de les remercier de leur conduite courageuse et exemplaire.

A. Panet, orateur

Wm. Lindsay, greffier, Ass.

Appendix C

De Salaberry in Literature

La Victoire de Châteauguay

La trompette a sonné : l'éclair luit, l'airain gronde;
Salaberry parait, la valeur le seconde,
Et trois cents Canadiens qui marchent sur ses pas,
Comme lui, d'un air gai, vont braver le trépas.
Huit mille Américains s'avancent d'un air sombre;
Hampton, leur chef, en vain veut compter sur leur nombre.
C'est un nuage affreux qui paraît s'épaissir,
Mais que le fer de Mars doit biéntôt éclaircir.
Le héros canadien, calme quand l'airain tonne,
Vaillant quand il combat, prudent quand il ordonne,
A placé ses guerriers, observé son rival :
Il a saisi l'instant, et donné le signal.
Sur le nuage épais qui contre lui s'avance,
Aussi prompt que l'éclair, le Canadien s'élance . . . . . .
Le grand nombre s'arrête . . . . . . il ne recule pas;
Il offre sa prière a l'ange des combats,
Implore du Très-Haut le secours invisible,
Remplit tous ses devoirs et se croit invincible.
Les ennemis confus poussent des hurlements;
Les chefs et les soldats font de faux mouvements.
Salaberry, qui voit que son rival hésite,
Dans la horde nombreuse a lancé son élite :
Le nuage s'entr'ouvre; il en sort mille éclairs;
La foudre et ses éclats se perdent dans les airs.
Du pâle Americain la honte se déploie :
Les Canadiens vainqueurs jettent des cris de joie;
Leur intrépide chef enchaîne le succès,
Et tout l'espoir d'Hampton s'enfuit dans les forêts.
Oui! généreux soldats, votre valeur enchante :
La patrie envers vous sera reconaissante.

Qu'un main libérale, unie au sentiment,
En gravant ce qui suit, vous offre un monument;
"Ici les Canadiens se couvrirent de gloire;
Oui! trois cents sur huit mille obtinrent la victoire
Leur constante union fut un rempart d'airain
Qui repoussa les traits du fier Américain.
Passant, admire-les . . . . . Ces rivages tranquilles
Ont été défendus comme les Thermopyles;
Ici Léonidas et ses trois cents guerriers
Revinrent parmi nous cueillir d'autres lauriers."

J.-D. Mermet
Spectateur, 25 November 1813

A Salaberry

Quoi! pas un mot pour te défendre!
Ta gloire, tes exploits, tout cela dans l'oubli!
Ton nom est-il enseveli
Pour toujours sous ta cendre?
Toi le héros de Châteauguay,
Toi, le vainqueur de la Pointe-aux-Erables,
Ces noms impérissables
Passeraient sans le tien à la postérité?

Chaque fois qu'on écrit l'almanach des grands hommes,
Déchire-t-on la page où brillait ton talent?
L'encre est-elle effacée, ou si le firmament
Qu'habite ton étoile échappe aux astronomes?
Où sont donc ces obus, ces bombes, ces boulets,
Dont les Américains ont senti la brûlure,
Et qui, sur leurs canons, gravait ta signature

Au bas de tes hauts faits!

Où sont-ils donc ces jours d'orgueilleuse mémoire
Où les feux du génie auréolaient ton front,
Et séduidaient Clio qui cousait a l'histoire
Le feuillet qu'elle fit pour illustrer ton nom?
Il était beau ce temps où tu voyais tout rose!
Voir au ciel, et pour nous l'horizon s'éclaircir,
Et contempler dans l'avenir
Le socle où son apothéose

S'élève grandiose,
N'est-ce pas l'idéal du bonheur, du plaisir?

Quand, de gloire enivrée, une jeunesse altière
Se ruait âme et corps sur les rangs ennemis
Qui cédant au courage allaient dans la poussière
    Former des monceaux de débris;
Ici, sous le plomb mortel qui rasait ton panache,
Tu marchais à la tête, et montrais le chemin
Où tes jeunes guerriers glanaient à pleine main
    Leur part des lauriers qu'on t'arrache.

Ces braves Voltigeurs, trempés à ton creuset,
Ils étaient beaux à voir sur le champ de bataille!
Demi-dieux par le coeur et géants par la taille,
Ils tordaient dans leurs bras l'Amérique en arret!

Quand la mort vint poser ses doigts nus et livides
Sur ton front où Bellone avait tracé des rides
    Et l'immortalité;
Quand ton âme, fuyant sa demeure argileuse,
S'élançait vers son Dieu pour prendre, radieuse,
    Sa place à son côté;
Vit-on nos citoyens, dans des groupes funèbres,
Se pencher sur la tombe et répandre des pleurs?
Ce jour fut-il inscrit parmi des jours célèbres,
    Dans le livre des coeurs?

Mais j'interroge en vain : depuis longtemps la place
N'était plus dans les coeurs qu'un vide, qu'un espace;
Le poète a jeté pour toi dans l'avenir
    De l'encens et du baume;
Mais l'histoire dira qu'un héros, un grand homme,
Trahit la liberté, qu'il aurait dû servir.

J. Phelan
La Minerve, 28 December 1835

Couplets

De notre pays les héros
Ont chasse les alarmes;

147

Il nous font goûter du repos
La douceur et les charmes.
Ces moments de paix
Ce sont leurs bienfaits,
Les fruits de leur courage.
Du pays l'honneur
Est de leur valeur
Et le prix et l'ouvrage.
De ma muse, Salaberry,
Daigne accepter l'hommage,
Dans tous nos coeurs ton nom chéri
Doit vivre d'âge en âge,
Briller désormais,
Rester à jamais,
Au temple de mémoire
La postérité
L'y verra gravé
Des mains de la victoire.
. . . . .
En vain l'Amérique enverra
Dans sa fureur altière,
Pour soumettre le Canada
Sa phalange guerrière;
Aux champs de l'honneur
Toujours la valeur
Peut braver sa puissance,
Quand Mars et Pallas
Pour guider nos pas
Semblent faire alliance.

Nos pères furent triomphants
Des horreurs de la guerre:
Puissent de leurs noms leurs enfants
Remplir aussi la terre.
Dans leur noble ardeur
De l'antique honneur
Toujours suivre la trace,
Encor plus heureux
Couronner nos voeux
Montrant la même audace.

Un Canadien
(Roy, p. 184)

Les Voltigeurs

Vous fûtes glorieux, jours de dix-huit cent douze,
Quand nos pères, grands coeurs qui battaient sous la blouse,
    Oubliant d'immortels affronts,
Sous les drapeaux anglais, en cohortes altières,
La carabine au poing, se ruaient aux frontières
    En chantant avec les clairons!

Gars à la joue imberbe, hommes aux mains robustes,
Toujours prêts à venger toutes les causes justes
    Comme à braver tous les pouvoirs!
Toujours prêts – ces héros – au premier cri d'alerte,
A répondre, arme au bras et la pointrine ouverte,
    A l'appel de tous les devoirs!

Regardez-les passer, ces guerriers d'un autre âge,
Conscrits dont le sang-froid, la gaieté, le courage
    Font honte au soldat aguerri!
Où vont-ils? Au combat! D'où viennent-ils? De France!
Comment s'appellent-ils? Ils s'appellent vaillance!
    Demandez à Salaberry.

Ce sont les Voltigeurs! Ils sont trois cents à peine;
Mais, vainqueurs d'une lutte ardente, surhumaine,
    Ils vont, de leur sang prodigues,
Sous des tombes de feu, riant des projectiles,
Un contre vingt, inscrire auprès des Thermopyles,
    Le nom rival de Châteauguay.

Avenir, saluez! saluez tous ces braves.
Leur héroïsme a su, repoussant les entraves
    Qu'on forgeait pour nos conquérants,
Rajeunir sur nos bords la légende de gloire,
Qui dit que lorsque Dieu frappe fort dans l'histoire,
    C'est toujours par la main des Francs.

Louis Fréchette
(Roy, p. 190)

Chambly

J'ai vu Chambly; j'ai vu sa Fertile campagne,
Sa rivière, ses bois et sa triple montagne.
J'ai vu dans ses jardins la déesse des fleurs
Aux charmes de Pomone unissant ses couleurs.
J'ai, sur ses flots d'argent, vu le canot fragile,
Aux couplets des rameurs, devenir plus docile.
Dans ce site attrayant, tout plaît et tout séduit,
Excepté le temps seul, qui trop vite s'enfuit.
J'ai vu briller partout les plus belles demeures;
J'ai tout compté, tout vu, mais sans compter les heures;
J'ai vu ses habitants, et tous m'ont répété
Que le plus doux devoir est l'hospitalité.
Toujours francs, toujours gais, ils m'ont offert l'image
Des hommes du vieux temps, des héros du bel âge.
C'est là que tout mortel n'obéit qu'à la loi
Et se donne a lui seul le beau titre de roi.
C'est là qu'un droit égal, une franchise extrême,
En montrant cent maisons, montre toujours la même.
Français de caractère, ils sont Anglais de coeur,
Et doublent leur patrie, en doublant leur bonheur.
C'est ainsi qu'autrefois, au sein de l'harmonie.
Fleurit des premiers grecs l'heureuse colonie.
J'ai vu, j'ai respecté le ministre du lieu;
Mon âme s'est élevée à l'autel du vrai Dieu;
Mais mon coeur des vertus dût admirer le temple.
Là j'ai vu l'homme heureux qui prêche par l'exemple:
Et chez lui j'ai connu cette pure amitié
Qu'en tout autre pays on ne voit qu'à moitié.
Héros et citoyen, tendre époux et bon maître,
Il est père de tous sans vouloir le paraitre.
Au camp Léonidas, aux champs Cincinnatus,
Thémistocle au conseil, a table Lucullus,
Sans avoir les défauts de la Grèce et de Rome,
Il réunit en lui les vertus du grand homme.
On voit à ses cotes, l'air pur, l'air grand, l'air gai;
L'air de Chambly s'y joint à l'air de Châteauguay.
On contemple, on admire et bientôt on s'amuse;
Le héros devient chantre et fait briller sa muse.
Son aimable compagne aux convives flattés
Présente l'ambroisie et porte des santés;

L'enfant avec douceur gesticule et sautille;
Et le bon mot succède au nectar qui pétille
Je me tais, mais où donc ai-je tant vu, tant ri?
Chacun le devine . . . . . . C'est chez Salaberry.

J.-D. Mermet
Roy, pp. 185-186

Notes

Chapter 1

1. The first siege took place in April and May, 1811, and the second in May and June of the same year.
2. D.J. Goodspeed, *The British Campaigns in The Peninsula 1808-1814* (Ottawa: Queen's Printer, 1958), p. 134.

Chapter 2

1. It was noted that "in every encounter with the bayonet, against Frenchmen, mulattoes, and negroes alike, we [the British] were successful." James Grant, *British Battles on Land and Sea* (London, Cassell & Co., n.d. [1874?]), p. 490.
2. In 1799 the island was renamed Prince Edward Island in honour of the Duke of Kent.
3. L.-O. David, *Biographies et Portraits* (Montreal: Beauchemin & Valois, 1876), p. 52.
4. W.D. Lighthall, *An Account of the Battle of Chateauguay* (Montreal: Drysdale, 1889), p. 11.
5. Devoe to Kent, October 1807 in de Salaberry Papers, P.A.C. MG 24 G45 Vol. 3 n.p.

Chapter 3

1. In later years, to ensure the succession of the British throne, the Duke of Kent was obliged to separate from his morganatic wife Mme. de St. Laurent and remarry. The child of this remarriage became Queen Victoria.
2. Kent to de Salaberry, 1 November 1808.
3. W.J. Anderson, *Canadian History and Biography* (Quebec: Middleton & Dawson, 1867), p. 23.

Chapter 4

1. David, *op. cit.*, p. 47. A magnificent combination of strength, dignity, vigour, and good looks; a powerful being overflowing with life and vitality. (My translation.)
2. Pierre-Georges Roy, *La Famille D'Irumberry De Salaberry* (Levis, Quebec: J.-A.K. Laflamme, 1905), p. 91-92.

Chapter 5

1. G. Stanley, "The Indians in the War of 1812", *Canadian Historical Review* Vol. XXXI no. 2 (June 1950).
2. This is the Pike of "Pike's Peak".

Chapter 6

1. Lighthall, *op. cit.*, p. 7.
2. S.E. Morison, *The Oxford History of the American People* (New York: Oxford University Press, 1965), p. 370.

Chapter 7

1. Hampton to Armstrong, Four Corners, 1 November, 1813.
2. Lighthall, *op. cit.*, p. 26. He lists the men who dove into the river to catch prisoners as privates Vincent, Pelletier, Vervais, Dubois, and Caron.

Chapter 8

1. Louis de Salaberry to Charles de Salaberry, 6 November, 1813. Quoted in Roy, *op. cit.*, p. 166.
2. This "eyewitness" was, in fact, Lt. Michael O'Sullivan. He later became a Chief Justice.
3. De Salaberry Letters, Vol. 1, p. 479.
4. Anderson, *op. cit.*, p. 33.
5. E. D'Aubreville to de Salaberry, Kingston, 26 March, 1814. De Salaberry Papers, Vol. 3.
6. Edward, Duke of Kent to Louis de Salaberry, 15 March, 1814. Quoted in J.P. Aubert de Gaspé, *Mémoire* (Quebec: N.S. Hardy, 1885).
7. Bathurst to Prevost, 27 December 1813 (italics mine).
8. De Salaberry Papers, Vol. 3, p. 1033. Charles de Salaberry to Louis de Salaberry, 24 January, 1814.
9. Roy, *op. cit.*, p. 167.
10. *Ibid.*, pp. 167-68.
11. *Ibid.*, pp. 168-69.
12. See Appendices.

Chapter 9

1. Roy, *op. cit.*, p. 176.
2. The medal was acquired by H.R.H. Princess Louise while her husband, the Marquess of Lorne, was Governor-General of Canada (1878-83). It was subsequently in the Herbert Eaton collection and bought at an auction in 1930 by Sir Albert Whittaker, C.B.E. The 60th Regiment attempted to buy it at the auction, but failed.
3. Robert la Roque de Roquebrune, *Hommage a Charles – Michel de Salaberry, Héros de Chateauguay* (Beloeil, Quebec: La Broquerie, 1913), p. 15.
4. De Salaberry Papers, Vol. 8, p. 1885.

Chapter 10

1. Now known as Mary, Queen of the World.
2. Viger, Vol. 60, p. 195.
3. Viger, Vol. 7B, p. 185.
4. *Ibid.*, p. 175.

Chapter 11

1. Roy, *op. cit.*, p. 121. He erroneously cites Alphonse's age as 57; it is a matter of record that Alphonse was born on 20 May, 1813 and died on 27 March, 1867.
2. The series of statues is completed by ones of Lévis, Talon, Marquette, Brébeuf, Dorchester, Baldwin, Elgin, Lafontaine, Boucher, La Vérendrye, Iberville, and Joliet.

Selected Bibliography

Manuscript Sources
Archives Nationales de Quebec
    AP-G 289 (Famille de Salaberry)
    AP-G 335 (Collection Baby)
    AP-G 417 (Collection Papineau)
Gagné, Lucien, C.S.S.R. *Salaberry 1778-1829.* Unpublished doctoral thesis, University of Montreal, 1948.
Public Archives of Canada
    K-134 (Louis de Watteville Journal)
    MG 24, G45 (De Salaberry Papers)
    MG 24, L8 (Saberdache de Jacques Viger)

Publications
American Military History 1607-1958. Washington: U.S. Department of the Army, 1959.
Anderson, W.J. *Canadian History and Biography.* Quebec: Middleton & Dawson, 1867.
_____. *The Life of F.M.H.R.H. Edward, Duke of Kent.* Ottawa: Hunter, Rose & Co., 1870.
Armstrong, John. *Notices of the War of 1812.* 2 vols. New York: Wiley and Putnam, 1840.
Aubert de Gaspé, J.P. *Mémoires.* Quebec: N.S. Hardy, 1885.
Auclair, E.-J. *Histoire De Châteauguay.* Montreal: Beauchemin, 1935.
Baby, L'Hon. Juge. "Châteauguay: Qui est 'Témoin Oculaire' et sa description de la bataille est-elle correcte?", *The Canadian Antiquarian and Numismatic Journal,* (April 1899) pp. 70-88.
A Brief History of The King's Royal Rifle Corps 1755-1948 3rd. ed. Aldershot, Gale and Polden Ltd., 1948.
Burt, A.K. *Guy Carleton, Lord Dorchester 1724-1808.* revised edition. Ottawa: Canadian Historical Association Historical Booklet #5, 1955.
Borthwick, J.D. *History and Biographical Gazeteer of Montreal to the Year 1892.* Montreal: D. Gallagher, 1892.
Brackenridge, H.M. *History of the Late War Between the United States and Great Britain.* Philadelphia: J. Kay, 1846.
Butler, Lewis. *The Annals of the King's Royal Rifle Corps.* vol. 1. London: Smith, Elder, 1913.
Cambridge History of the British Empire. Cambridge, England: Cambridge University Press, 1930.
Cambridge History of British Foreign Policy. Cambridge, England: Cambridge University Press, 1922.
Cambridge Modern History. Cambridge, England: Cambridge University Press, 1906.
Christie, Robert. *The Military and Naval Operations in the Canadas.* Quebec: Oram & Mott, 1818.

Coffin, W.F. *1812 – The War and Its Moral*. Montreal: J. Lovell, 1864.

Cruikshank, E.A. *The Documentary History of the Campaign Upon the Niagara Frontier in the Year 1813*. 9 vols. Welland, Ont: Lundy's Lane Historical Society, 1896-1908.

_____. "The Employment of Indians in the War of 1812", *American Historical Association Annual Report, 1895*. Washington: 1896.

David, L.O. *Biographies et Portraits*. Montreal: Beauchemin et Valois, 1876.

_____. *Lt.-Col. Charles Michel de Salaberry*. Montreal: Desbarats, 1872.

_____. *Le Héros de Chateauguay*. Montreal: Cadieux et Derome, 1883.

Desloges, Yvon, "La Naissance d'un Mythe", *Conservation Canada*, 1 (2) Ottawa: Parks Canada, 1974.

De Salaberry Thérèse. *Regards sur la Famille d'Irumberry de Salaberry*. Paris: Editions de L'Orante, 1953.

Des Ormes, R. "Evocations des Salaberry", *Revue de L'Universite Laval*, IV, (2), October 1949.

Fortesque, J.W. *The History of the British Army*. vol. iv. London: Macmillan Co., 1906.

Garneau, F.X. *Histoire du Canada VII*. Montreal: Editions de l'arbre, 1945.

Goodspeed, D.J. *The British Campaigns in the Peninsula 1808-1814*. Ottawa: Queen's Printer, 1958.

Grant, James. *British Battles on Land and Sea*. London: Cassell & Co., N.D. (1874?).

Hannay, James. *History of the War of 1812*. Toronto: Morang, 1905.

Hopkins, J. Costell. *French Canada*. Toronto: Bell and Cockburn, 1913.

Irving L.H. *Officers of the British Forces in Canada During the War of 1812-15*. Welland, Ont: Welland Tribune Print., 1908.

James, Wm. *A Full and Correct Account of the Military Occurances of the Late War etc-*. London: Wm. James Pub. 1818.

Lighthall, W.D. *An Account of "The Battle of Chateauguay" (a lecture at Ormstown, March 8, 1889)*. Montreal: W. Drysdale & Co., 1889.

Lossing, B.J. *Pictorial Field Book of the War of 1812*. New York: Harper and Brothers, 1869.

Lucas, C.P. *The Canadian War of 1812*. Oxford: Henry Frowde, 1906.

MacKay Hitsman, J. *The Incredible War of 1812: a military history*. Toronto: University of Toronto Press, 1965.

Mahan, A.T. *Sea Power and Its Relation to the War of 1812*. 2 vols. New York: Greenwood, 1968.

Mahon, John K. *The War of 1812*. Gainesville, Fla.: University of Flordia, 1972.

Morgan, Henry J. *Biographies of Celebrated Canadians*. London: Hunter Rose Co., 1862.

Morrison, Samuel, Eliot. *The Oxford History of the American People*. New York: Oxford University Press, 1965.

Pratt, J.W. *Expansionists of 1812*. New York: Macmillan Co., 1925.

Provencher, Champlain. *Le Héros de Châteauguay*. Montreal: (no publisher), 1902.

Roper, Jim. "The Battle of Chateauguay", *The Blue Bell*. Bell Canada, October, 1963.

Roquebrune, Robert le Roque de. *Hommage à Charles-Michel de Salaberry, Héros de Châteauguay*. Beloeil, Quebec: La Broquerie, 1913.

Roy, P.G. *La Famille D'Irumberry de Salaberry*. Levis, Quebec: J.-A.K. Laflamme, 1905.

_____. *Old Manors, Old Houses*. Quebec: King's Printer, 1927.

Stacey, C.P. *The Military Problems of Canada*. Toronto: Ryerson Press, 1940.

Stanley, G.F.G. *Canada's Soldiers 1604-1954*. Toronto: Macmillan Co., 1954.

_____. "The Indians in the War of 1812", *Canadian Historical Review*. XXXI (2), June 1950.

Sulte, Benjamin. *La Bataille de Châteauguay*. Quebec: Demers, 1899.

_____. *Histoire de la Milice Canadienne Francaise*. Montreal: Desberats, 1897.

Waugh, Alec. *A Family of Islands: A History of the West Indies*. New York: Doubleday, 1964.

Illustration and Photograph Credits

Page 11   Portrait by Don G. McNab, Château Ramezay Museum, Montreal
Page 12   Photograph by Judy Wohler
Page 16   Photograph by Leslie Titcombe
Page 20   Sketch by David Garvin
Page 22   Photograph courtesy of Parks Canada
Page 33   *The Annals of the King's Royal Rifle Corps*, 1913, p. 248
Page 42   Journal of the Society for Army Historical Research, Vol. x,
           No. 40 (Oct. 1931) p. 237
Page 47   Map by the author
Page 54   Photograph courtesy of Parks Canada
Page 58   Photograph by the author
Page 69   Map by the author
Page 74   Map by the author
Page 82   Sketch map from an old illustration by David Thompson
Page 85   Public Archives of Canada
Page 91   Photograph courtesy of Parks Canada
Page 96   Sketches by Eugene Lelièpvre, courtesy of Parks Canada
Page 98   Sketches by Eugene Lelièpvre, courtesy of Parks Canada
Page 102   Sketches by Eugene Lelièpvre, courtesy of Parks Canada
Page 106   Sketches by Eugene Lelièpvre, courtesy of Parks Canada
Page 111   Photograph courtesy of Parks Canada
Page 121   Photograph courtesy of Parks Canada
Page 124   Sketch by David Garvin
Page 129   Public Archives of Canada
Page 133   Photograph by Judy Wohler
Page 135   National Museums of Canada
Page 137   Photograph by Judy Wohler
Page 139   Photograph by Judy Wohler

Index